International Labour and Employment Compliance Handbook

www.kluwerlawonline.com

Labour and Employment Compliance in The United Kingdom

International Bar Association

Labour and Employment Compliance in The United Kingdom

Second Edition

Ed Mills
Ailie Murray
Anna West
Gareth Walls
Emmie Ellison
Elliot English

This publication is part of the International Labour and Employment Compliance Handbook, available on www.kluwerlawonline.com

Editors: Salvador del Rey and Robert J. Mignin
Associate Editor: Juan Bonilla

the global voice of the legal profession

Wolters Kluwer

Published by:
Kluwer Law International B.V.
PO Box 316
2400 AH Alphen aan den Rijn
The Netherlands
E-mail: international-sales@wolterskluwer.com
Website: lrus.wolterskluwer.com

Sold and distributed by:
Wolters Kluwer Legal & Regulatory U.S.
7201 McKinney Circle
Frederick, MD 21704
United States of America
E-mail: customer.service@wolterskluwer.com

ISBN 978-94-035-3904-1

e-Book: ISBN 978-94-035-3905-8
web-PDF: ISBN 978-94-035-3910-2

All listed titles are also available on lrus.wolterskluwer.com

1. Argentina: Julio César Stefanoni Zani & Enrique Alfredo Betemps, *Labour and Employment Compliance in Argentina, 9th edition*, 2021 (ISBN 978-94-035-3622-4)
2. Australia: John Tuck, Stephen Price, Rosemary Roach, Jack de Flamingh, Nicholas Ellery & Nick Le Mare, *Labour and Employment Compliance in Australia, 6th edition*, 2021 (ISBN 978-94-035-3914-0)
3. Belgium: Chris Van Olmen, *Labour and Employment Compliance in Belgium, 6th edition*, 2021 (ISBN 978-94-035-3602-6)
4. Brazil: Rodrigo Seizo Takano, Andrea Giamondo Massei & Murilo Caldeira Germiniani, *Labour and Employment Compliance in Brazil, 8th edition*, 2021 (ISBN 978-94-035-3625-5)
5. Canada: Kevin Coon & Adrian Ishak, *Labour and Employment Compliance in Canada, 2nd edition*, 2014 (ISBN 978-90-411-5637-2)
6. Chile: Gerardo Otero A., María Dolores Echeverría F., María de los Ángeles Fernández S. & Javier Sabido, *Labour and Employment Compliance in Chile, 9th edition*, 2021 (ISBN 978-94-035-3635-4)
7. China: King & Wood Mallesons, *Labour and Employment Compliance in China, 6th edition*, 2021 (ISBN 978-94-035-3894-5)
8. France: Pascale Lagesse, *Labour and Employment Compliance in France, 9th edition*, 2021 (ISBN 978-94-035-3672-9)
9. Germany: Gerlind Wisskirchen & Martin Lützeler, *Labour and Employment Compliance in Germany, 9th edition*, 2021 (ISBN 978-94-035-3605-7)
10. India: Manishi Pathak, *Labour and Employment Compliance in India, 9th edition*, 2021 (ISBN 978-94-035-3662-0)
11. Ireland: Duncan Inverarity & Ailbhe Dennehy, *Labour and Employment Compliance in Ireland, 8th edition*, 2021 (ISBN 978-94-035-3911-9)
12. Israel: Pnina Broder-Manor, Helen Raziel & Ilan Winder, *Labour and Employment Compliance in Israel, 8th edition*, 2021 (ISBN 978-94-035-3612-5)
13. Italy: Angelo Zambelli, *Labour and Employment Compliance in Italy, 9th edition*, 2021 (ISBN 978-94-035-3642-2)
14. Japan: Yoshikazu Sugino, *Labour and Employment Compliance in Japan, 9th edition*, 2021 (ISBN 978-94-035-3632-3)
15. Republic of Korea: Sang Wook Cho, Soojung Lee & Christopher Mandel, *Labour and Employment Compliance in the Republic of Korea, 7th edition*, 2021 (ISBN 978-94-035-3645-3)
16. Mexico: Oscar De La Vega Gómez, *Labour and Employment Compliance in Mexico, 9th edition*, 2021 (ISBN 978-94-035-3615-6)
17. The Netherlands: Els de Wind & Cara Pronk, *Labour and Employment Compliance in the Netherlands, 4th edition*, 2018 (ISBN 978-94-035-0470-4)
18. Poland: Barbara Jóźwik, *Labour and Employment Compliance in Poland, 9th edition*, 2021 (ISBN 978-94-035-3675-0)
19. Russia: Anna-Stefaniya Chepik, *Labour and Employment Compliance in Russia*, 2013 (ISBN 978-90-411-4925-1)

20. Saudi Arabia: Sara Khoja & Sarit Thomas, *Labour and Employment Compliance in Saudi Arabia, 4th edition,* 2021 (ISBN 978-94-035-3652-1)
21. South Africa: Susan Stelzner, Stuart Harrison, Brian Patterson & Zahida Ebrahim, *Labour and Employment Compliance in South Africa, 9th edition,* 2021 (ISBN 978-94-035-2773-4)
22. Spain: Salvador del Rey, Ana Campos & Sergi Gálvez Duran, *Labour and Employment Compliance in Spain, 9th edition*, 2021 (978-94-035-3665-1)
23. Turkey: Sertaç Kökenek & Elif Nur Çakır Vurgun, *Labour and Employment Compliance in Turkey, 7th edition*, 2021 (ISBN 978-94-035-3901-0)
24. United Arab Emirates: Sara Khoja & Sarit Thomas, *Labour and Employment Compliance in the United Arab Emirates, 8th edition*, 2021 (ISBN 978-94-035-3655-2)
25. United Kingdom: Ed Mills, Ailie Murray, Anna West, Gareth Walls, Emmie Ellison & Elliot English, *Labour and Employment Compliance in The United Kingdom, 2nd edition*, 2021 (ISBN 978-94-035-3904-1)
26. United States: Andrew J. Boling, Amy de La Lama, William Dugan, Chris Guldberg, Brian Hengesbaugh, Robert J. Mignin, Virginia Mohr, John M. Murphy & Ginger Partee, *Labour and Employment Compliance in the United States, 6th edition*, 2020 (ISBN 978-94-035-2813-7)

International Bar Association
The Global Voice of the Legal Profession

The International Bar Association (IBA), established in 1947, is the world's leading organization of international legal practitioners, bar associations and law societies. The IBA influences the development of international law reform and shapes the future of the legal profession throughout the world. It has a membership of over 40,000 individual lawyers and almost 200 bar associations and law societies spanning all continents. It has considerable expertise in providing assistance to the global legal community.

Grouped into two divisions – the Legal Practice Division and the Public and Professional Interest Division – the IBA covers all practice areas and professional interests, providing members with access to leading experts and up-to-date information. Through the various committees of the divisions, the IBA enables an interchange of information and views among its members as to laws, practices and professional responsibilities relating to the practice of business law around the globe. Additionally, the IBA's high-quality publications and world-class conferences provide unrivalled professional development and network-building opportunities for international legal practitioners and professional associates.

The IBA's Bar Issues Commission provides an invaluable forum for IBA member organisations to discuss all matters relating to law at an international level.

The IBA's Human Rights Institute (IBAHRI) works across the Association, to promote, protect and enforce human rights under a just rule of law, and to preserve the independence of the judiciary and the legal profession worldwide.

Other institutions established by the IBA include the Southern Africa Litigation Centre and the International Legal Assistance Consortium.

Employment and Industrial Relations Law Committee

The aims of the committee are to develop and exchange knowledge of employment and industrial relations law and practice. Members support each other through the provision of innovative ideas and practical assistance on day-to-day issues. In addition, through its journal and through presentations, conferences, the committee ensures the dissemination of up-to-date law and practice in this highly important business area.

International Bar Association Global Employment Institute

The IBA Global Employment Institute (IBA GEI) was formed in early 2010 for the purpose of developing for multinationals and worldwide institutions a global and strategic approach to the key legal issues in the human resources and human capital fields.

Drawing on the resources and expertise of the IBA membership, the IBA GEI will provide a unique contribution in the field of employment, discrimination and immigration law, on a diverse range of global issues, to private and public organizations throughout the world. The IBA GEI is designed to enhance the management, performance and productivity of these organizations and help achieve best practice in their human capital and management functions from a strategic perspective.

The IBA GEI will become the leading voice and authority on global HR issues by virtue of having a number of the world's leading labour and employment practitioners in its ranks, and the support and resource of the world's largest association of international lawyers.

Further information

International Bar Association, 4th Floor, 10 St Bride Street, London EC4A 4AD, United Kingdom, Tel: +44 (0)20 7842 0090, Fax: +44 (0)20 7842 0091, E-mail: member@int-bar.org, www.ibanet.org

About the International Labour and Employment Compliance Handbook

From 1976 through 1988, the International Bar Association and Kluwer Law International published the groundbreaking International Handbook on Contracts of Employment. This Handbook provided one of the first global overviews of the law of the international employment relationship.

Since publishing the first edition, globalization of business has created an increased demand for knowledge of labor and employment laws throughout the world. Therefore, along with Kluwer, we decided to publish an updated Handbook which we have titled the International Labour and Employment Compliance Handbook.

This new Handbook was intended to be a practical guide by providing a general overview of key labor and employment issues in multiple jurisdictions. Each chapter was written so that it is easy to understand by lawyers and non-lawyers alike. Each country author has also followed a standard outline to assist readers in analysing employment issues in each country.

The first edition of this new Handbook included nineteen (19) different countries.

This Handbook would not have been possible without the help and assistance of many people. Most importantly, the individual country authors are all distinguished legal practitioners who spent considerable time drafting and revising their country reports to meet difficult deadlines. We thank each of them. Our friends at Kluwer, especially Ewa Szkatula, have done a wonderful job in keeping the editors and the authors on schedule. Finally, we want to also express our gratitude to Cuatrecasas, Gonçalves Pereira, and Baker & McKenzie LLP for their valuable assistance in the coordination and organization of this project. Our warmest thanks to each of them.

Because of the success of the Handbook,Wolters Kluwer Law & Business decided to publish each country report also as a separate book to give a choice in obtaining the information. We hope this new format will be a helpful and useful resource just like the Handbook. Both formats are available in print and online.

The Editors

Salvador del Rey Guanter
Robert J. Mignin

March 2013

Table of Contents

United Kingdom

AUTHORS

Ed Mills

Ed Mills is a Partner and Head of the Employment Department at Travers Smith LLP where his practice covers the full range of contentious and non-contentious employment law issues as well as business immigration.

Ed advises clients on a broad range of employment issues including board level disputes, team moves, discrimination, Transfer of Undertakings (Protection of Employment) Regulations 2006 (TUPE), collective consultation, trade union issues and litigation in the Employment Tribunal and the High Court. He also advises on business immigration issues including sponsorship under the UK Visas and Immigration (UKVI) 'points-based system'. Ed has significant experience in conducting and advising on complex investigations, often involving whistleblowing disclosures and cross-border issues.

He is recognized by Chambers and Partners for his wide range of employment work and is listed as a 'Leading Individual'.

Ed is also a member of the Employment Lawyers Association (ELA), the European Employment Lawyers Association (EELA), the American Bar Association (ABA) and the International Bar Association (IBA) for whom he is a regular conference speaker.

Ailie Murray

Ailie is a Senior Counsel in the Employment Department at Travers Smith and is a dual Scots and English law qualified solicitor.

Ailie advises clients on all aspects of employment law and has a specific focus on corporate transactions and restructurings. She has significant experience advising clients on the employment aspects of complex, often multi-jurisdictional, acquisitions and disposals, including private equity investments. Her role frequently involves coordinating overseas employment advice, particularly in relation to employee transfers, changing terms and conditions and workforce reductions. She assists clients to navigate through the complexity of multiple legal frameworks and works with them to develop multi-jurisdictional strategies.

Ailie is an active member of the EELA and the International Association of Young Lawyers (AIJA).

Anna West

Anna is a Knowledge Counsel in the Employment Department at Travers Smith.

Anna helps to keep the Employment team and its clients up-to-date on employment law changes and best practices. She regularly devises and presents seminars and training sessions, both internally for the team and externally for clients' HR teams, managers and staff. Anna has a particular interest in discrimination, family-friendly issues and collective consultation.

Anna is a member of the ELA and sits on the ELA Training Committee. She is also a member of the Professional Support Lawyers Employment Network.

Gareth Walls

Gareth Walls is Partner & Head of the Employment Department at A&L Goodbody (Belfast Office).

Gareth regularly advises employers, regulated entities and public bodies on all aspects of employment law in Northern Ireland. He is recognized by both Chambers UK and Legal 500 as 'one of the best employment lawyers in Northern Ireland' and is particularly well regarded for his advisory work on TUPE (and the Service Provision Change Regulations as they apply in Northern Ireland). He also has experience in advising on all aspects of contentious employment work and is an experienced advocate in the courts and tribunals of Northern Ireland.

Emmie Ellison

Emmie is a solicitor in A&L Goodbody's Employment Practice Group in Belfast. She advises both private and public sector, domestic and international clients in relation to a variety of contentious and non-contentious employment law issues. Emmie has been recognized in Legal 500 for having 'the ability to distil complex legal issues'.

Elliot English

Elliot is a solicitor in A&L Goodbody's Employment Practice Group in Belfast. He advises on a variety of contentious and non-contentious employment law issues and assists in Corporate Immigration and Visa matters.

ADDRESS

Travers Smith LLP
10 Snow Hill
London
EC1A 2AL
Tel.: +44(0)207 295 3000
E-mail: ed.mills@traverssmith.com
Web: www.traverssmith.com

A&L Goodbody
42/46 Fountain Street
Belfast
BT1 5EF
Tel.: +44 28 9031 4466
E-mail: gwalls@algoodbody.com
Web: www.algoodbody.com

COVID-19 Information

The UK Government adopted various measures to support employers and employees in response to the COVID-19 pandemic.

Coronavirus Job Retention Scheme

In March 2020, the Coronavirus Job Retention Scheme (CJRS) was introduced. Under the CJRS employees can be 'furloughed', which means that they cannot carry out any work for their employer. The Government pays 80% of the monthly wages of furloughed employees (up to a cap of GBP 2,500 per month). Employers can top the employee's pay up but are not obliged to do so. Initially, any furlough period was required to last at least three weeks, but this no longer applies since the introduction of 'flexible' furloughing (*see* below). Furlough periods may be extended, and employees may be brought back and then re-furloughed.

Due to the ongoing pandemic, the CJRS is set to continue until 30 September 2021 (extended from the original closure date of 31 October 2020). On 1 July 2020, a system of 'flexible' furloughing was introduced which allows employees to perform some work while furloughed. From 1 May 2021, employees can only be furloughed if they were on the employer's PAYE payroll from 2 March 2021. The employer must pay employees in full for the hours worked, but furlough pay is available for normal hours not worked. The system will be gradually wound down with the government contribution reducing to 70% and 60% at the start of July and August, respectively. Employers must make up the difference to ensure the employees receive 80% of their monthly wage (capped at GBP 2,500 per month).

Business Loans

The Government also introduced a series of business loans to support businesses during the pandemic. Depending on the prospective borrower's annual turnover and needs, they were eligible to apply for loans under either the:

- Bounce Back Loan Scheme ('BBLS') for businesses of any turnover, providing loans of up to GBP 50,000;
- Coronavirus Business Interruption Loan Scheme ('CBILS') for businesses with an annual turnover of up to GBP 45 million, providing loans of up to GBP 5 million; or
- Coronavirus Large Business Interruption Loan Scheme ('CLBILS') for businesses with an annual turnover of over GBP 45 million, providing loans of up to GBP 200 million.

Loans under the BBLS are for six years (although there is no penalty for early repayment). Loans under CBILS are for (i) up to six years for term loans and asset finance and (ii) up to three years for overdrafts and invoice finance.

The UK Government provides the lender with a guarantee for either 80% (under CBILS and CLBILS) or 100% (for BBLS) of the outstanding loan meaning it is more likely to be approved by the lender. The UK Government pays the first twelve months of interest on behalf of borrowers for loans under the CBILS and BBLS (but not the CLBILS).

The schemes are operated through accredited lenders (including most high-street banks) of the British Business Bank. The UK Government loan guarantees are only to the lender, so the borrower remains fully liable to repay 100% of the debt (including any interest). However, borrowing under the CBILS or BBLS was particularly attractive to businesses facing a short-term cash-flow issue in view of the interest-free element. The BBLS, CBILS and CLBILS closed to new applicants on 31 March 2021.

On 6 April 2021, the UK Government introduced the Recovery Loan Scheme (RLS) to provide further support to businesses who can apply for a loan of up to GBP 10 million. The Government guarantees 80% of the finance to the lender. The maximum length of the facility is up to three years for overdrafts and invoice finance facilities, or up to six years for loans and asset finance facilities. The RLS is open until 31 December 2021.

Legal Compliance in the United Kingdom

1. LEGAL FRAMEWORK: EMPLOYMENT LAWS

Employment law in the UK has three main sources:

(1) Contract: The relationship between the employer and the employee is governed at common law by the contract of employment. Certain terms are implied into all employment contracts, including the mutual duty of trust and confidence.
(2) Legislation: A range of statutes and statutory instruments confer a number of minimum statutory rights on employees. The key statutes in Great Britain (GB) are the Employment Rights Act (ERA) 1996 and the Equality Act (EqA) 2010. In Northern Ireland, a key piece of legislation is the Employment Rights (Northern Ireland) Order 1996 and there is also a range of applicable anti-discrimination legislation (with each protected ground addressed within a distinct piece of legislation).
(3) European law: Most European derived employment laws have been implemented in the UK in domestic legislation, but there are a few which are directly applicable, such as the General Data Protection Regulation (GDPR) (*see* further below for a discussion of the implications of Brexit on European derived laws).

Most employment laws apply to England/Wales, Scotland and Northern Ireland in the same way, although there are a few differences, and these are stated where relevant in the sections below.

2. CONTRACTS OF EMPLOYMENT

2.1. Overview

A contract of employment sets out the employment relationship between the employee and employer. It can be either oral or in writing, although the ERA, section 1, requires employers to provide employees and workers with a written statement of certain particulars of employment (*see* below).

A contract of employment will generally consist of:

(1) express terms, which are explicitly agreed between the parties, either in writing or orally;
(2) implied terms, which are those taken to have been agreed under common law because:
    (a) they are too obvious to need recording;
    (b) they are part of the custom and practice of the business or industry;
    (c) they can be logically deduced from the conduct of the parties;
    (d) they are necessary to give 'business efficacy' to the agreement as a whole; or
    (e) they are implied under employment legislation.
(3) terms incorporated into individual contracts from other sources, such as collective agreements with a trade union.

2.2. Written Employment Contracts

Written Employment Contracts

A written contract of employment is more common than an oral contract. Written employment contracts will typically contain express terms and incorporate the particulars required under section 1 ERA. A written contract may comprise several different documents including a written statement of particulars, offer letter and employee handbook.

Written Particulars of Employment

Employers are required to provide a statement of initial particulars to all workers in accordance with section 1 ERA. This statement must be provided on or before the date on which employment starts; although particulars relating to pensions, collective agreements, training, and disciplinary and grievance procedures can be given in instalments but no later than two months after the start of employment. Before 6 April 2020, employers were required to provide only the employees (not workers) with an initial statement of particulars within two months of the beginning of employment, and this is still the period which applies in Northern Ireland.

Some particulars must be included in a single document, and others can be given by reference to other reasonably accessible documents. A summary of the particulars required to be in a single document is set out below:

- Names of the employer and employee/worker.
- Date on which employment began.
- Date on which period of continuous employment began.
- Intervals at which remuneration is paid.
- Place of work.
- Job title or description.
- Any terms and conditions relating to hours of work.
- Any terms and conditions relating to holidays.
- Period for which employment is expected to continue or the end date (for fixed-term employment).
- Details of terms and conditions for working abroad and those relating to the return to the UK (where the employee is required to work outside the UK for a period of more than one month).
- Any other benefits provided by the employer.
- Any training requirements.
- Conditions and duration of any probationary period.

An employer must also provide details of other particulars in writing, but they are not required to be contained within a single document. These particulars include disciplinary and grievance procedures (including details of how and to whom the employee can appeal in respect of any disciplinary or grievance decision) and the terms and conditions relating to paid leave.

Changes to any of the particulars must be given to the employee or worker in writing within one month of the change.

Typically the statement of particulars will be incorporated into a written employment contract, which will satisfy section 1 ERA if it is given before or on the date on which employment commences.

If there is no separate written contract of employment, the statement of particulars can evidence the terms of employment agreed between the parties. If there is a separate written contract it will take precedence over the statement of particulars.

Where an employer is in breach of the duty to give a written statement of particulars or particulars of change, the Employment Tribunal is obliged to make an award of two weeks' pay and may, if it considers it just and equitable, award four weeks' pay (subject to the statutory limit which is currently GBP 544 per week and increases annually every April). This award will only be made if the employee is successful in a specific claim including, but not limited to, equal pay, discrimination, unlawful deductions from wages, unfair dismissal and breach of contract.

In Northern Ireland, the written statement of particulars should be provided within two months of an employee commencing employment; however, it is a good practice to provide this as soon as possible.

2.3. Oral Contracts

Although oral contracts are legally enforceable, it is better to have a written contract as evidence of the express terms that have been agreed between the parties and to satisfy the requirement for written particulars under the ERA (*see* above). Also, post-termination restrictive covenants must be in writing to be enforceable (*see* section 15 below).

2.4. Employee Handbooks

It is common practice to have an employee manual or handbook which contains policies and procedures that are applicable to employees. An employer will need to consider whether the contents of the handbook should have contractual effect and form part of the terms and conditions of employment. Most employee handbooks or manuals will consist of non-contractual policies so that they can be amended and updated without obtaining the consent of the employees, employees and, depending on the employer's business sector, may need to be considered alongside a relevant regulatory compliance manual.

The requirements under section 1 ERA specify that for some particulars the statement may simply cross-refer to a separate policy or document. It is not uncommon for statements of particulars or contracts of employment to refer to an employee handbook to satisfy this condition.

2.5. Job Descriptions

There is no requirement to provide an employee with a job description (except in some financial services roles). However, the written particulars under the ERA must include the employee's job description or a brief description of the work for which they are employed.

2.6. Offer Letters

Often an employer will prepare an offer letter to set out conditions precedent, such as satisfactory references, right to work in the UK, qualifications, background/criminal record checks and there being no restrictive covenants preventing the employment. Typically, an offer letter will also contain key information about the role including the job title, term of appointment and starting salary. Sometimes an offer letter will enclose a copy of the employment contract for the employee to sign before or when they commence work.

If the offer letter itself is to comprise the entire contract of employment, then it is important to check that the offer letter contains all the relevant terms of employment and particulars required under section 1 ERA. It should expressly incorporate any other document that may contain contractual terms (e.g., an employee handbook.)

If the offer letter is to be superseded by a separate written contract of employment, then the employer should make the offer of employment conditional upon the signing of the full contract and acceptance of its terms.

The contract of employment should make it clear that in the event of any inconsistency, it is the contract terms that will prevail. It may also be useful to include an 'entire agreement' clause in the offer letter and/or contract which records that the document contains the entire agreement as to the employee's terms of employment (if this is the case) as this will prevent an employee subsequently arguing that they are entitled to contractual terms other than those set out in the offer letter or contract. For the same reason, it may be advisable to include a provision in the offer letter or contract stating that the employee has not relied on any oral or written representations which are not contained in the offer letter or contract.

2.7. Checklist of Dos and Don'ts

- Ensure that all employees sign a contract of employment which clearly sets out the terms and conditions of the employment relationship.
- Ensure that all workers and employees are provided with a written statement of particulars that complies with section 1 ERA before or on the date on which employment starts. These particulars may take the form of a contract of employment.
- If an offer letter is issued it should include the conditions of the offer and make it clear whether the offer letter will form part of the contract of employment or if a separate contract of employment is to follow.

- Consider whether an employee handbook or manual contains contractual terms that should form part of the contract of employment or whether it contains non-contractual policies and procedures.
- Even if there is no staff handbook in place, ensure that certain procedures, such as disciplinary, grievance and equal opportunities policies and procedures are drafted and made accessible to employees.

3. RECRUITING, INTERVIEWING, SCREENING AND HIRING EMPLOYEES

3.1. Overview

Effective recruitment procedures enable employers to recruit the very best employees while reducing the risks of litigation. Such procedures require an objective, systematic and planned approach to recruitment if unlawful discrimination is to be avoided. Both short-listing and selection should be on the basis of candidates' relevant experience, skills, qualifications, knowledge and talent, and should be based on factual evidence.

Note that certain advertising requirements apply if an employer is recruiting an individual who will need immigration sponsorship (*see* section 14 below).

3.2. Recruiting

There is no statutory framework specifically governing the recruitment process in the UK. However, it is unlawful to discriminate against a candidate during the recruitment process. Discrimination is unlawful if it is based on race, sex, disability, age, religion/belief, sexual orientation, gender reassignment, pregnancy/maternity or marital/civil partner status.

An employer must not discriminate against a candidate in the way it operates the recruitment process, or in the terms on which it offers employment, or by rejecting the candidate.

A candidate could bring a discrimination claim against the employer and/or any employees or recruitment agents if they were involved in the alleged discrimination or harassment. It is therefore advisable that employers devise and implement recruitment procedures, training and guidelines for all staff involved in the process of recruitment, and have clear policies and agreements with any recruitment agents.

In Northern Ireland the Fair Employment and Treatment (Northern Ireland) Order 1998 applies and provides that it is unlawful to discriminate in respect of an applicant's, or an employee's religious belief and/or political opinion and such claims will be dealt with via the Fair Employment Tribunal in Northern Ireland. For further information in respect of ensuring active practice of fair employment in Northern Ireland, refer to section 24.

3.3. Employment Applications

The two most common forms of application are the curriculum vitae (with a covering letter) or a standard application form produced by the employer. The advantage of application forms is that the employer can control the type of information that is collected and restrict such information to that which is relevant to the position being applied for. Application forms also ensure that everyone competes at the same level. Candidates may be invited to apply for a job directly through an advertisement or jobs website, or the employer may use a recruitment agent or headhunter to search for candidates.

3.4. Pre-employment Inquiries

Most employers will carry out certain specific background checks in relation to prospective employees who have been offered a job (*see* section 3.6 below), many of which involve checking information which the employee has volunteered. Employers may carry out wider vetting of candidates (e.g., internet searches or speaking to mutual contacts) but for data protection reasons this should only be done where the role justifies this more extensive information gathering.

3.5. Pre-employment Tests and Examinations

Aptitude tests (such as computer skills) should always relate to the skills required to perform the offered employment. Language skills may need to be tested where proficiency in a language is a requirement for a particular role.

Employers are increasingly using psychometric testing, which tests aspects of personality and intelligence, or biodata that tests biographical data. Thought needs to be given as to whether tests such as these are necessary and proportionate, will involve any invasion of privacy, how feedback may be given, and how the data generated is to be stored. These tests should not be the sole method of assessment and all candidates will need to be informed in advance, either verbally or in writing, if these are to be used as testing methods.

Under the EqA 2010 (section 60) the employer must not ask about the health of a job applicant before making an offer of employment, except to:

- ask about a health matter which is intrinsic to the role (e.g., asking a candidate for a driving role whether they have any health condition which means they are unable to drive);
- ask whether there are any reasonable adjustments which the candidate needs to be made to the recruitment process.

After offering the job, the employer may ask health questions and/or ask the prospective employee to undergo a medical check, but the information sought should be limited to that which is relevant to the role.

The EqA 2010 does not apply in Northern Ireland and as such, employers in Northern Ireland (or those with employees based in Northern Ireland) should refer to section 4 of the Disability Discrimination Act 1995 and the Equality Commission Northern Ireland (ECNI) for guidance in this respect. The ECNI guidance suggests that employers should only seek information from job applicants and employees about their health when there is an objectively justifiable reason for doing so. In particular, employers should consider what reasonable adjustments may be required and final selection decisions should only follow an assessment of how the applicant would perform in the job if these reasonable adjustments were actually made.

3.6. Background, Reference and Credit Checks

In the financial services sector, employers are required to obtain detailed references for their regulated employees, and are obliged to provide a reference if requested by another employer for a regulated role.

Outside the financial services sector, there is no general legal obligation on an employer to obtain or to provide a reference, but it is common practice to do so. However, many employers will only provide a limited reference which confirms the individual's dates of employment and the role that they held.

In addition to seeking references, an employer may choose to verify factual data provided by the employee such as academic or professional qualifications, for example, by seeing original certificates.

Some employers seek pre-employment credit checks. These checks should be proportionate and justified in relation to the role applied for. It is likely to be appropriate to carry out credit checks for a role that involves the prospective employee handling cash or accounts or working for a financial institution (where this may also be a regulatory requirement).

Most employers carry out criminal record checks. For most roles, only a basic criminal records check is justified. This reveals details of any convictions which are not yet 'spent' (most convictions become 'spent' after a certain number of years which means they do not need to be revealed in a job application). For some roles, including many legal and accountancy roles, the employer can obtain a standard criminal record check which includes details of spent as well as unspent convictions, and in certain roles involving work with children or vulnerable adults, employers can obtain an enhanced criminal records check which contains detailed information from police records. Any criminal records checks must be carried out in accordance with data protection laws (*see* section 26 below). The process for carrying out criminal record checks in Scotland is in the process of being amended following the introduction of the Disclosure (Scotland) Act 2020. As of the date of writing, the changes have not yet been implemented.

The Rehabilitation of Offenders (Northern Ireland) Order 1978 applies in Northern Ireland. In Northern Ireland there is an official criminal history disclosure service known as AccessNI which is operated by the Department of Justice. AccessNI is the official source of information and provides guidance about the legal duties that employers must comply with in relation to employing former offenders. AccessNI is used frequently for those working with vulnerable people, for example, those working with children in schools.

Employment offers should be made conditional on satisfactory references and other checks.

3.7. Interviewing

Employers may ask any questions they like at interview provided that they do not ask any potentially discriminatory questions, for example, questions asked of a female candidate are not asked of a man, such as those concerned with plans to have children. To avoid the risk of claims of discrimination, it is good practice for interviewers only to ask questions which relate to the candidate's ability to do the job, and such questions should be asked consistently of all candidates. It is advisable to keep notes of interviews in case of any future discrimination claim.

3.8. Hiring Procedures

Careful notes should be kept of any decisions made by the manager who is carrying out the recruitment exercise, to assist with the defence if any discrimination claim is brought at a later date.

Employers should ensure that employees sign a contract before commencing employment, and that satisfactory references have been received, checks made regarding credit records, criminal records and qualifications (where appropriate) and that proof has been obtained that employees have a right to work in the UK.

Through the application form or CV, pre-screening checks and interview process, the employer will receive a great deal of personal data, including special category data, from job applicants. The employer will need to ensure that it handles this data in accordance with data protection laws and will need to think carefully about what it will do with it when the recruitment process has come to an end (*see* section 26 below).

3.9. Fines and Penalties

The Equality and Human Rights Commission (EHRC) can issues a notice, and ultimately a fine for non-compliance, against an employer for a discriminatory advertisement.

If an employer is found to be liable for an act of discrimination, they can be ordered to pay compensation to the complainant, and there is no limit to the compensation that can be ordered (*see* section 17 below).

An employer will also be liable to a civil penalty if it negligently employs someone who does not have permission to work in the UK. There is a statutory defence if the employer checks certain documents before the employment starts and (in some cases) at least every twelve months during employment. In addition, an employer will commit a criminal offence if it knowingly employs someone who does not have permission to work in the UK (*see* section 14 below).

3.10. Checklist of Dos and Don'ts

- Consider carefully the criteria or requirements for each role and whether they could potentially have an indirect discriminatory impact or may narrow the pool of candidates who may apply.
- Consider having a system for receiving applications that allows the employer to control the amount and type of information sought, such as a standard application form.
- Adopt a recruitment policy that sets out the procedures to be followed in connection with advertising posts, short-listing, interviewing, etc.
- Consider the pre-employment checks that are necessary for the post being recruited, and ensure that the offer is conditional on these being satisfactory.
- Retain any documents which document the decision-making process in relation to an individual, so that the employer can justify any decision made should a complaint or litigation be brought.

4. MANAGING PERFORMANCE/CONDUCT

4.1. Overview

Poor performance and misconduct are both issues that an employer can expect to face from time to time with employees. If an employee is dismissed, they may challenge the fairness of that process in the employment tribunal if the employer has not acted fairly and reasonably in dealing with the employee. Effective performance/conduct management procedures can therefore mitigate the risk of a claim being brought against employers.

Disciplinary and capability procedures enable employers to set a framework within which managers can address and improve conduct and poor performance issues in the workplace.

It is implied in every employment contract that an employee will perform their role with reasonable skill and care. This will vary from role to role and can encompass not only the technical aspects of the employee's role but also subjective aspects such as their attitude, ability to interact with colleagues and clients.

Informal discussions may be enough to notify an employee that their conduct or performance is not meeting the required standard. Any warnings given at this stage should be verbal, strictly informal and not form part of an employee's disciplinary record or considered in future proceedings. This is because formal warnings should only be issued where a fair procedure has been followed (*see* section 4.4 below).

4.2. Coaching and Counselling

Some employers may offer employees coaching or counselling either on an informal basis, without starting a formal performance management procedure or as part of the formal process.

4.3. Written Evaluations

Most employers have a system of appraisals (often on an annual basis but sometimes more frequently) that assist with the identification of performance issues at an early stage, but there is no legal obligation on them to do so. An appraisal is a two-way process between an employee and employer during which targets and objectives are set – and areas of improvement highlighted.

4.4. Warnings and Suspensions

Except where an employee commits an act of gross misconduct (i.e., conduct which is serious enough to justify immediate dismissal without warnings) or gross negligence, the disciplinary/capability procedure should provide a system of warnings, and time for the employee to improve. Failure to follow a fair performance/conduct procedure could result in an unfair dismissal. Employees must have two years' service to bring an unfair dismissal claim, but it is nevertheless important to follow a clear procedure in relation to all employees, as failure to do so could assist an employee who claims that discrimination or whistleblowing is the real reason for dismissal (there is no service requirement for either of these claims).

The Advisory, Conciliation and Arbitration Service (ACAS) has published a statutory Code of Practice on discipline and grievances at work, setting out the procedures which should be followed. In summary, a fair procedure requires the employer to inform the employee of the concerns about their performance or conduct, and hold a meeting with them at which they can discuss the concerns (and they may bring a colleague or trade union representative to the meeting), before issuing a warning. The employee must also have the right to appeal against any warning. A failure to comply with this Code may lead to an increase of up to 25% on any compensation awarded in an unfair dismissal claim.

In Northern Ireland, employees must have one year of service to bring an unfair dismissal claim. The conciliation body in Northern Ireland (equivalent to ACAS in England, Wales and Scotland) is known as the Labour Relations Agency (LRA). It makes similar recommendations to ACAS in respect of managing performance and conduct (as outlined above) and these are contained in the LRA Code of Practice on Disciplinary and Grievance procedures.

In instances of serious misconduct, an employer may wish to suspend the employee who is being investigated. This may be appropriate, for example, where there is a potential threat to the business or to other employees, or when it is not possible to properly investigate the allegation if the employee remains at work (e.g., because the employee may destroy evidence or attempt to influence witnesses). Suspension must be justified, and if an employer suspends an employee unnecessarily, it could undermine the mutual trust and confidence between the employer and employee and leave an employee with a right to resign and claim constructive dismissal. Any period of suspension should be as short as reasonably possible, the decision to suspend should be kept under review, and it should be made clear that suspension is not considered a disciplinary action. Unless there is a clear contractual provision to the contrary, suspension should be on full pay.

4.5. Checklist of Dos and Don'ts

- Conduct regular evaluations of employees to give an honest assessment of their performance and allow them to raise any concerns.
- Ensure performance and conduct management processes are conducted in line with the company's policies and the ACAS Code of Practice.
- Keep accurate records of action, including informal action, taken against employees.
- When issuing warnings for non-performance, implement a system of reviews, coaching and training in appropriate cases.

5. TERMINATION OF EMPLOYEES FOR PERFORMANCE OR DISCIPLINARY REASONS

5.1. Overview

Employees with at least two years' continuous service are protected against being unfairly dismissed by their employer. In summary, in order for an employer to show that they have fairly dismissed an employee, they must demonstrate that they have: (a) a fair reason for the dismissal; and (b) followed a fair process.

Fair Reasons

The following can be potentially fair reasons for an employer to dismiss an employee:

- misconduct;
- lack of capability or qualifications (which would include poor performance);
- redundancy;
- illegality (i.e., it would be illegal to continue to employ the individual); or
- 'some other substantial reason' (SOSR). SOSR may be used where the reason for dismissal does not fall neatly into one of the other potentially fair reasons for dismissal. This could include a fixed-term contract ending or (in some cases) where there has been a complete breakdown in trust and confidence between the employer and employee.

A dismissal for any reason which is not one of the above potentially fair reasons will be unfair. An employer must also act reasonably and fairly in treating that reason as a reason for dismissal.

Conduct Dismissals

Misconduct could include either a single act of serious misconduct or a series of acts that are less serious. Most employers include examples of unacceptable misconduct in their employment contracts and/or staff handbooks.

It may be fair to dismiss an employee for conduct outside the workplace if it affects the employer or could be thought to affect employee performance. For example, becoming involved in a fight outside work while wearing a uniform that would identify the employer, or making offensive or derogatory comments on social media where employees have identified themselves as being affiliated with their employer.

To ensure that a dismissal on the grounds of conduct is fair, the employer must be able to show that, at the time of the dismissal:

- it genuinely believed the employee to be guilty of misconduct;
- it had reasonable grounds for believing that the employee was guilty of that misconduct; and
- when it formed that belief on those grounds, it carried out a reasonable investigation.

Performance/Capability Dismissals

When deciding if an employer has acted reasonably in dismissing an employee for poor performance, the tribunal will need to consider factors such as:

- whether the employee knew what was required;
- whether the employer provided training, supervision and encouragement;
- whether it warned the employee of the consequences of failing to improve and gave them a chance to improve; and
- in some cases, whether the employer considered alternative employment.

When a determination is made about whether a dismissal is fair, the Tribunal will consider whether the employer has followed the ACAS Code of Practice on disciplinary and grievance procedures (*see* section 4 above). A failure to do so could lead to an increase of up to 25% in the compensation awarded to the employee in an unfair dismissal claim.

In Northern Ireland an employee gains unfair dismissal protection once they have completed one year's continuous service. In Northern Ireland there is a statutory dismissal procedure as outlined in Schedule 1 of the Employment (Northern Ireland) Order 2003. This procedure provides that an employer must:

- issue the employee with a 'statement of grounds for action' and invite the employee to a meeting to discuss same;
- hold the meeting with the employee (once they have had a reasonable opportunity to consider their response to the information provided) and issue an outcome after the meeting (which must also notify the employee of their right of appeal); and
- after the outcome has been issued, afford the employee a right of appeal, if this is requested.

Employers in Northern Ireland should also seek to follow the LRA code of practice on disciplinary and grievance procedures for a best practice approach.

5.2. Separation/Severance Pay

Employers are always required to provide notice of termination under the employee's contract, or payment in lieu of notice, unless the employee was dismissed in the circumstances justifying immediate termination without notice (e.g., gross misconduct).

If the employer faces a potential claim of unfair dismissal, it may choose to offer the employee an ex gratia or lump sum settlement payment to compensate them for the unfair dismissal. In these circumstances, the employee should be asked to sign a settlement agreement, waiving any right to bring statutory employment claims (*see* section 25 below).

5.3. Fines and Penalties

If an employee is found by an Employment Tribunal to have been unfairly dismissed, the employer may be ordered to pay compensation. The maximum compensation that can be awarded for unfair dismissal is a basic award (based on age and length of service) of up to GBP 16,320 together with a compensatory award consisting of the lower of twelve months' salary or the statutory cap (currently GBP 89,493 and increased every April). Compensation may also be increased by up to 25% where the employer has failed to follow the ACAS code (although still subject to the statutory cap).

In Northern Ireland, if an employee has been unfairly dismissed a claim may be made to the Industrial Tribunal of Northern Ireland, and as of 6 April 2021 the statutory cap for the compensatory award for a successful unfair dismissal claim is GBP 88,669 (this limit increases every year), or one year's salary (whichever is lower). This does not include the basic award which will be calculated based on the employee's age, length of service and weekly pay. If the employer fails to follow the statutory procedure, where it applies and an employee, who is qualified to do so, makes a claim for unfair dismissal, the Industrial Tribunal will find the dismissal automatically unfair. The Tribunal will normally increase the compensation awarded by between 10% and 50% where it feels it is just and equitable to do so.

5.4. Checklist of Dos and Don'ts

- Have a disciplinary policy in place setting out the procedure to be followed when an employee is faced with disciplinary issues.
- Include a non-exhaustive list of examples of gross misconduct in the disciplinary procedure or contract of employment.
- Have a performance management/appraisal system in place to identify, and act on, poor performance issues at an early stage.
- Conduct a thorough investigation and carry out a fair process (in accordance with the ACAS code) prior to dismissing employees for misconduct or capability.
- Keep good records and documentation relating to any disciplinary action taken against employees and of any performance discussions with employees.

6. LAYOFFS, REDUCTIONS IN FORCE, AND/OR REDUNDANCIES AS A RESULT OF JOB ELIMINATIONS OR OTHER RESTRUCTURING

6.1. Overview

Employers must follow a fair redundancy procedure involving individual consultation, in order to avoid a claim for unfair dismissal. In addition, where the employer is making twenty or more redundancies within a ninety-day period, the rules on collective redundancy consultation will apply. Breach of the collective consultation provisions can give rise to separate claims and penalties over and above those arising from any unfair dismissal.

6.2. Reductions in Force/Layoffs/Job Eliminations

An employee will be redundant, and entitled to a statutory redundancy payment (*see* below), where the employer has a reduced requirement for employees to carry out work of a particular kind, for example, where there is a headcount reduction, or deletion of certain roles, or a closure of a site or business division. In UK law, a lay-off is different from a redundancy. An employee is laid off where they are not given work for a particular period, but they remain employed (*see* further below in relation to lay-offs).

Individual Redundancy Consultation

In order to ensure that a dismissal for redundancy is fair, an employer must follow a fair redundancy procedure involving:

- Warning employees about the proposed redundancies.
- Using a fair basis upon which to select employees for redundancy (an employer must identify the correct pool from which to select potentially redundant employees and must select employees using reasonable criteria).
- Considering suitable alternative employment within the organization.
- Consulting employees at each stage of the process.

In order to be reasonable, selection criteria must, as far as possible, be both objective and capable of independent verification, and should relate to the role, such as performance, skills and experience.

Unless an employer is obliged to engage in collective consultation (as described below) there are no prescribed timescales within which consultation should take place, but it will typically take two to four weeks in straightforward cases.

Collective Redundancy Consultation

There is a duty to collectively consult where an employer proposes to dismiss as redundant twenty or more employees at one establishment within a period of ninety days or less. This collective consultation should start before the individual consultation process, and some aspects of the collective and individual consultation process may run in parallel. However, redundancy termination notices should not be issued until the collective consultation has finished.

For these purposes:

- 'proposing' means more than merely contemplating making the potential redundancies but entering into consultation before the decision has been made;
- the definition of 'dismiss as redundant' is slightly wider than the standard definition of redundancy (*see* above) and means any termination of an employment contract where the reason for the dismissal does not relate to the individual employee concerned. Such definition would bring not only traditional redundancy dismissals within its scope but also dismissals, for

example, where an employer proposes to dismiss employees who have not agreed to a change to their contracts of employment.

The duty is to inform and consult appropriate representatives of the 'affected employees' (i.e., those affected by the proposed dismissals or by other measures which the employer proposes to take in connection with the dismissals, for example, altering shift patterns).

If a trade union is recognized by the employer (*see* section 9 below), the employer must consult trade union representatives about the redundancies. Otherwise, the employer may consult with an existing employee body such as a works council, if it represents all the affected employees, or invite employees to elect representatives in a ballot (which has to meet certain requirements).

Certain minimum time periods for the consultation apply, depending on the scale of the redundancies proposed. Where one hundred or more redundancies are proposed, consultation must begin at least forty-five days before the first dismissal takes effect. For twenty to ninety-nine proposed redundancies, the consultation period has to begin thirty days before the first dismissal.

Consultation begins with the provision of information (specified by statute) on the proposals to representatives. Consultation must be undertaken with a view to reaching an agreement on ways to avoid the dismissals, reducing the number of dismissals and mitigating their consequences.

Where the duty applies, the employer must also notify the Government Insolvency Service of the proposed redundancies (at least forty-five days before the first dismissal if one hundred or more redundancies are proposed, and at least thirty days before the first dismissal if twenty to ninety-nine redundancies are proposed). Failure to do so is a criminal offence and, if convicted, the employer will be liable to an uncapped fine, and individual directors may also face criminal liability.

Alternatives to Redundancy: Layoffs and Short-Time Working

As an alternative to making employees redundant, an employer may wish to deal with an unexpected downturn in its business or unforeseen circumstances by laying off employees or putting them on short-time working, that is, requiring employees to work fewer hours than they are contracted for – commonly a four, three or even a two day week. Employees remain employed during the lay-off period, making this an attractive option for employers as it immediately provides a saving in labour costs coupled with the flexibility to restore the workforce when a trade starts to pick up.

Some employers anticipate the need to lay off employees or to put them on short-time working by including an express right to do so in employment contracts. Others operate within industries where, through custom and practice of laying off employees or putting them on short-time working, the employer has an implied right to do so. Employees have the right to receive a guarantee payment during lay-off of GBP 29 per day for up to five days in any three-month period.

If an employer lays off an employee or puts them on short-time working in the absence of an express or implied right to do so, the employer will be in fundamental breach of contract, entitling the employee to resign and claim constructive dismissal. If the reason for dismissal is redundancy, which is probable in this situation, the employee may also claim a statutory redundancy payment after four weeks of lay-off or short-term working, or six weeks in any thirteen-week period. Alternatively, an employee with insufficient service to bring a redundancy pay or unfair dismissal claim, or who does not wish to do so, may remain in employment and claim any shortfall in wages by means of a deduction from wages claim.

The UK Government has brought in a temporary wage subsidy scheme in response to the coronavirus pandemic. The CJRS started on 1 March 2020 and is set to run to 30 September 2021 and permits employers to 'furlough' employees, i.e., keep them off work, on 80% of their wages (capped at GBP 2,500 per month) and reclaim this from the Government (with the Government contribution reducing in the last three months of the scheme, to 70% of wages in July and 60% in August and September).

Northern Ireland

Where an employer is proposing to dismiss as redundant twenty or more employees at one establishment within a period of ninety days or less, the employer must consult the employee representatives about the dismissals. The consultation must begin in good time and in any event, at least ninety days before the first dismissal takes effect where the employer is proposing to dismiss one hundred or more employees; otherwise, at least thirty days before the first dismissal takes effect. An employer must notify the Department of Economic Development of such collective redundancies in accordance with these timescales.

If there is no express right to lay off or place an employee on short-time working, an employer should seek the employee's consent before implementing such measures. During lay-off or short-time working an employee may be entitled to statutory guarantee payments. The maximum an employee can claim is GBP 30 per day (this limit increases annually) for five days in any three-month period. Failure to make such payments may result in the employee bringing an unlawful deduction to wage claim.

If an employee has been placed on lay-off or short-time working (earning less than half of their weekly wage) for four consecutive weeks or six weeks within a thirteen-week period, they are entitled to give their employer written notice that they intend to claim redundancy pay.

The employer then has seven days to either accept the claim or give the employee a written counter-notice. The counter-notice is to inform the employee that the notice for redundancy pay is not accepted because work will be available within the next four weeks which will last at least thirteen weeks without interruption. If no counter-notice is issued the employer is assumed to have accepted the employee's claim.

6.3. Fines and Penalties

Redundancy Payments

Employees with a least two years' continuous employment are entitled to a statutory redundancy payment if they are dismissed by reason of redundancy.

Statutory redundancy pay is calculated according to a formula based on age, length of service and pay. The maximum number of years that may be taken into account to calculate a redundancy payment is twenty years. Further, for these purposes, a week's pay is capped at the statutory maximum, currently GBP 544.00 (the cap increases in April each year). The maximum statutory redundancy payment for 2021/2022 is GBP 16,320.

Employees may also be entitled to enhanced redundancy payments through an express contractual entitlement (e.g., their employment contract or a collective agreement) or an implied entitlement as a result of established custom and practice.

Unfair Dismissal

Employees with two years' continuous service or more can bring a claim of unfair dismissal if their employer has acted unreasonably in making them redundant. In practice, complaints will generally be about a lack of consultation, failure to follow a fair procedure, selection decisions and process and not offering alternative jobs where available. The maximum compensation that can be awarded by an employment tribunal for unfair dismissal is the lower of twelve months' salary or the statutory cap. The cap for 2021/2022 is GBP 89,493 (this cap increases in April each year).

Breach of Collective Consultation Procedures

Failure to comply with the collective consultation requirements can lead to what is known as a 'protective award' being made by an employment tribunal. The maximum protective award is up to ninety days' pay per dismissed employee. This is gross pay, and the statutory cap on a week's pay does not apply. The award is not based on loss of earnings, but on the seriousness of the employer's default. The seriousness will vary from a mere technical breach to a complete failure to inform and consult. Where there has been no consultation at all, it is appropriate for the tribunal to start with the maximum protective award and then examine whether there are any mitigating circumstances which would justify the award being reduced.

Failure to Notify the Secretary of State

Failure to provide the notification of collective redundancies to the Secretary of State is a criminal offence, and an employer is liable to an unlimited fine. Individual directors may also be prosecuted and face criminal liability.

Northern Ireland

In Northern Ireland one weeks' statutory redundancy pay is capped at GBP 566. Employees with one years' continuous service or more can bring a claim of unfair dismissal. The maximum compensation that can be awarded by an industrial tribunal for unfair dismissal is the lower of twelve months' salary or the statutory cap. The current statutory cap for the compensatory award in 2021/2022 is GBP 88,669. This does not include the basic award which is also payable should an employee be successful in bringing an unfair dismissal claim. Failure to provide the notification of collective redundancies to the Department of the Economy is an offence, and an employer is liable on summary conviction to a fine not exceeding level 5 on the standard scale.

6.4. Checklist of Dos and Don'ts

– Identify the number of proposed redundancies at an early stage so that the correct procedures can be adopted, and in order to assess whether the collective consultation rules are likely to apply.
– Plan the redundancy process carefully but be prepared to be flexible if necessary.
– Allow sufficient time for meaningful consultation. Discuss the reasons for the redundancies as well as other issues such as selection.
– Consider carefully the appropriate pool of employees from which selections for redundancy are to be made, including whether the pool should also incorporate other employees who do a similar job or have similar skill sets.

- Give careful thought to selection criteria. Do not use criteria which are too subjective, or which might indirectly discriminate, e.g., on the grounds of sex or disability.

7. LABOUR AND EMPLOYMENT LAW RAMIFICATIONS UPON THE ACQUISITION OR SALE OF A BUSINESS

7.1. Overview

The labour and employment law ramifications upon the acquisition or sale of a business depend on whether the transaction is structured as a business and asset transfer or a share transfer.

Business and Asset Transfer

On a business and asset transfer, in the majority of cases, the employees will transfer from being in the employment of the seller to being employed by the buyer as a result of the application of the Transfer of Undertakings (Protection of Employment) Regulations 2006 ('TUPE').

TUPE applies where there is a 'relevant transfer', which is the transfer of a business, or part of a business or where there is a transfer of an economic entity that retains its identity. A 'relevant transfer' also covers outsourcing arrangements, such as the contracting-out of in-house services, switching contractors or transferring services back in-house. This is in each case known as a service provision change.

Share Transfer

On a share transfer, usually there will be no change in the identity of the employer of the employees in the business (i.e., they remain employed by the entity being sold or acquired). As a result, from a legal perspective, the employees experience very little change on a share sale or acquisition. However, TUPE may apply on share sale if there is a pre- or post-sale reorganization which involves a business or asset transfer.

This chapter focuses on the application of TUPE, considering this primarily from the perspective of the buyer on the acquisition of a business and the perspective of the seller on the sale of a business.

7.2. Acquisition of a Business

Automatic Transfer

Where TUPE applies, all individuals employed by the seller immediately prior to the transfer, who are 'assigned to the organised grouping of resources or employees that is subject to the relevant transfer' will automatically transfer into employment with the buyer, with their accrued employment rights and continuity of employment intact. Any employee who would have been employed had they not been dismissed because of the transfer or a reason connected with it, will also automatically transfer to the buyer.

The automatic transfer principle does not apply to self-employed workers, agency workers or any employee who is only temporarily assigned to the grouping of resources or employees.

Protection from Dismissal

The buyer cannot dismiss any of the transferring employees unless the reason for the change is unrelated to the transfer or there is an economical, technical or organizational reason which involves a headcount reduction (e.g., redundancy) or a change in the functions performed by the transferring employees (an economic, technical or organizational (ETO) reason). Any transfer-related dismissal that is not for an ETO reason will be automatically unfair (although the two-year service requirement for bringing an unfair dismissal claim still applies).

Terms and Conditions of Employment

Transferring employees transfer on their existing terms and conditions of employment. Any changes to terms and conditions will be void, if the sole or principal reason for the change is the transfer itself, unless either the reason for the change is an ETO reason.

There are a few areas to be aware of as follows:

- Pensions: old age, invalidity and survivor's benefits under occupational pension scheme rights do not transfer under TUPE. However, the buyer is obliged to offer minimum pension benefits to transferring employees and any obligation in an employment contract to pay a percentage of salary into a transferring employee's personal pension will transfer. The exception does not apply to other benefits under an occupational pension scheme, which are not old-age, invalidity or survivor's benefits. For example, any early retirement benefits or enhanced redundancy will transfer.

- Incentives and Benefits: certain categories of incentives or benefits, by their nature, may not be transferable. For example, the transferring employees may be eligible to participate in the seller's group employee share option scheme or the seller may provide bespoke staff discounts and it may not be possible for the buyer to continue or replicate the incentives or benefits. In such circumstances, the buyer will be required to provide the transferring employees with substantially equivalent incentives or benefits. What amounts to substantially equivalent will depend on the specific incentive or benefit. Alternatively, the buyer may have to buy out those employees' rights.
- Restrictive Covenants: while restrictive covenants also transfer with the rest of the contract, as they will be interpreted and construed as at the time the contract was entered into, they will relate seller's business, not the buyer's. Depending on the particular circumstances of the case, it may be necessary for the buyer to arrange for the restrictive covenants to be amended, but this will be subject to the buyer's limited rights to make changes to the contract and will require consideration. Note that in Scotland, there is no requirement for consideration to be provided to amend restrictive covenants.
- Collective Terms: Any trade union collective or recognition agreements relating to transferring employees will continue to apply to the buyer (although the buyer may be entitled to terminate these agreements following the transfer).

Accrued Rights and Liabilities

All of the seller's rights, powers, duties and liabilities under or in connection with the transferring employees' contracts pass to the buyer. In addition, the buyer will inherit all outstanding employment liabilities connected with the employees (e.g., unpaid wages or bonuses), and any acts or omissions of the seller before the transfer are treated as having been done by the buyer (including any acts and omissions which can give rise to unfair dismissal claims, discrimination or equal pay claims). In other words, there is a statutory novation of employment contracts and the buyer steps into the seller's shoes in respect of all the transferring employees.

However, while it is not possible to exclude or contract out of TUPE, frequently the business transfer agreement may contain indemnities given by the seller in favour of the buyer in respect of any pre-transfer liabilities relating to the employees.

Objections

Transferring employees can object to the TUPE transfer. If they object, their employment terminates automatically on the date of the transfer without any pay in lieu of notice or compensation.

Transferring employees can also resign and claim unfair dismissal if the transfer would involve a substantial change in their working conditions to their material detriment, e.g., it would involve working at a location very far away from the employee's home.

Due Diligence

Before an acquisition takes place, the buyer should undertake a due diligence process, whereby it will try to obtain as much information as possible about the employees and other workers in the business. This usually involves the buyer submitting a questionnaire to the seller asking for certain information and/or confirmations, which among other things, will include the following:

- A list of all employees and workers of the business, together with details of their terms and conditions of employment (including copies of relevant agreements), salary, incentive arrangements and benefits.
- Details of any employees considered key to the business, which usually includes management, together with copies of their employment contracts and details of current remuneration. In particular, the buyer will usually want to understand what protections they have again these employees leaving the business following the sale or transfer and joining a competitor (e.g., notice periods, restrictive covenants). If necessary, changes to terms and conditions (to the extent possible) or other incentives, may need to be negotiated.
- Details of any recognized trade union or other employee representative bodies and/or collective bargaining agreements.
- Details of any existing or potential disputes with the employees or workers.
- Confirmation that the employer has complied with all its legal obligations relating to the employees and workers (e.g., paying national minimum, providing holiday entitlement).

The information should be provided in a manner that complies with relevant data protection legislation.

7.3. Acquisition Checklist

On the acquisition of a business, the buyer should:

- determine whether the transfer will trigger the application of TUPE and if, as a result, they will inherit any existing employees of the business;
- carry out a thorough due diligence process to establish which employees may transfer under TUPE, what terms and conditions they are engaged on and what liabilities may transfer with them;
- determine what 'measures' they are intending to take in relation to the employees who are to transfer, including changing any terms and conditions of employment or making redundancies, and notify the seller of any such proposed measures to enable them to consult with the employees (*see* section 7.4 below); and
- be cautious of dismissing any employee in connection with a transfer under TUPE as it may be found to be automatically unfair.

7.4. Sale of a Business

Employee Liability Information

TUPE imposes a duty on the seller of a business or assets to provide to the buyer with certain information about the transferring employees, their terms and conditions of employment and associated liabilities. This is known as 'employee liability information' and consists of:

- the identity and age of the employees who will transfer;
- information contained in those employees' written particulars of employment under section 1 ERA 1996 (*see* section 2);
- information on any collective agreements affecting those employees which will still have effect after the transfer;
- any disciplinary proceedings taken against an employee or grievance brought by an employee in the previous two years;
- any legal actions taken by those employees against the seller in the previous two years, and any such potential legal actions where the seller has reasonable grounds to believe such actions might occur.

This information must be provided to the buyer at least twenty-eight days in advance of the transfer.

In Northern Ireland, employee liability information is required no later than fourteen days before the date of transfer.

Information and Consultation

On the sale of a business, TUPE requires the seller to inform and, in some circumstances, consult with employees who will be affected by the transfer of the business. Affected employees are not only the transferring employees but can also include members of the seller's ongoing workforce or the buyer's existing workforce (post-transfer). Therefore, this obligation can also apply to the buyer.

Information

Employers must provide employee representatives with details of:

- the timing of and reasons for the TUPE transfer;
- the implications of the transfer for the affected employees (including its effect on their contracts of employment, remuneration and benefits, etc.);
- any 'measures' envisaged in connection with the transfer, by either the buyer or seller, relating to the affected employees. Measures are not defined in TUPE. However, measures have been interpreted very widely and can cover any action, step or arrangement which may impact on an affected employee's day-to-day working life, including any proposed changes to terms and conditions or benefits of proposed redundancies. The buyer must provide the seller with information about any measures it envisages to enable the seller to pass the information to employee representatives; and
- information about agency workers working anywhere in the employer's business, including the number of agency workers, the areas of the business in which they are working, and the type of work they are carrying out.

TUPE requires the information to be provided to employee representatives long enough before the transfer to enable the necessary consultations to take place.

Consultation

In addition to their duty to inform, the seller and the buyer are under a duty to consult employee representatives if, in relation to any of their affected employees, they will be taking any measures in connection with the transfer. If no measures are envisaged, the employee representatives must be notified accordingly and no duty to consult will arise. In practice, the duty to consult is rarely triggered because usually the buyer will be taking measures in relation to the seller's employees after the transfer, but neither buyer nor seller will be taking any measures in relation to their own employees.

TUPE states that the aim of the consultation process should be to seek the agreement of the employee representatives as to the measures to be taken in relation to the transfer. However, the representatives have no right of veto to prevent the TUPE transfer from taking place or to prevent measures from being implemented.

Appropriate Representatives

An employer's duties under TUPE are to inform and consult employee representatives who are:

- recognized trade union representatives; or
- employee representatives elected by the workforce.

Businesses with fewer than ten employees are exempt from electing representatives. They may discharge their obligation to inform and consult by informing and consulting the affected employees directly.

Northern Ireland

The applicable legislation in Northern Ireland is the Transfer of Undertakings (Protection of Employment) Regulations 2006 and the Service Provision Change (Protection of Employment) Regulations (Northern Ireland) 2006. In Northern Ireland information and consultation must always take place via elected reps, regardless of the number of affected employees, so the exemption for businesses with fewer than ten employees does not apply.

Failure to Comply

The maximum sanction which can be awarded by a Tribunal against an employer who has failed properly to comply with the duties to inform and/or consult is thirteen weeks' actual pay per employee.

7.5. Sale Checklist

On the sale of a business, a seller should:

- determine whether the transfer will trigger the application of TUPE and if, as a result, the employee engaged in that business will automatically transfer with the business to the buyer. If TUPE does not apply, the employees will remain employed by the Seller unless an agreement can be reached with both the employee and the buyer to transfer their employment;
- gather the employee liability information on all the employees to be transferred to the buyer and ensure the information is provided to the buyer no later than twenty-eight days before the transfer;
- inform representatives of affected employees about the transfer and consult with them if any measures are proposed. In order to comply with

this requirement, the seller should ensure that the buyer has provided them with details of any measures they intend to take; and
- be cautious of dismissing any employee in connection with a transfer under TUPE as it may be found to be automatically unfair.

8. USE OF ALTERNATIVE WORKFORCES: INDEPENDENT CONTRACTORS, CONTRACT EMPLOYEES, AND TEMPORARY OR LEASED WORKERS

8.1. Overview

There are three types of legal relationship which arise under English employment law:

(1) Employed
(2) Self-employed
(3) Worker.

A worker is an individual who is not an employee but is not in business on their own account, as a self-employed individual is. An example would be a casual or zero-hours worker, who does not have an employment contract with one employer but takes on individual assignments on an ad hoc basis, and often for several different organizations. There are also agency workers, who may be employed or engaged by the agency, and will be sent by the agency to work at the agency's client organizations.

Employees have the greatest protections under employment law; self-employed individuals have the fewest. Workers have many of the same rights as employees but not all. Most notably, workers cannot claim unfair dismissal.

8.2. Independent Contractors

8.2.1. Definition

The term 'independent contractor' is commonly used to describe someone who is truly self-employed. Broadly, someone who is truly self-employed will work for one or more organizations which will be clients of the individual's business.

There is no statutory definition of self-employment, but case law has developed a number of factors which are relevant to deciding whether an individual is employed or self-employed. These include:

- Control: an employee will be subject to the employer's control over what work is done, and how, and when and where.
- Personal service: if the individual can send a substitute to work in their place then this would be a strong indicator of self-employment (although in practice many self-employed individuals would not be permitted to send a substitute, particularly if they are providing a skilled or specialist service).
- Other activities: an employee will usually be restricted from working for others as employers expect exclusive service, but a self-employed individual will often provide services to more than one organization.
- Financial risk: if the individual takes any risk of financial loss, like payment by commission only or a lump sum payment for completing a project (regardless of how long it takes), this indicates self-employment; in contrast an employee would not usually take any financial risk (other than in respect of variable bonus or commission pay) and would receive a regular wage or salary.
- Integration: if the individual is integrated into the workforce, for example, reporting into team structures and attending team meetings and social events, this would tend to indicate employment rather than self-employment.
- Expenses: reimbursement of expenses is suggestive of an employment relationship, whereas a self-employed person would be expected to bear their own expenses.
- Pension/benefits: a self-employed person would usually not be expected to participate in the pension scheme, or be entitled to other benefits like medical insurance, whereas it is common to provide these for an employee.
- Sick pay: someone who is self-employed will usually only be paid for the work they do and would not be paid during any periods when they are not working, including sickness absence, whereas an employee would receive statutory sick pay (SSP) and possibly also enhanced company sick pay.
- Holiday – a self-employed individual would usually only be paid for the work they do, and would not be given any paid holiday, in contrast to employees who will be given paid holiday (of at least the statutory minimum and often more).

The Employment Tribunal will look at the whole picture, including what happens in practice as well as the terms of any written contracts, to decide whether an individual is an employee or self-employed.

A self-employed contractor may provide the services directly to the client organization, or through a personal services company owned by the contractor. If the contractor supplies services through a personal services company, then it is unlikely that they would be regarded as an employee of the client organization for the purposes of employment law.

The use of a personal services company also affects the tax position. If a directly engaged contractor is not genuinely self-employed, but more properly regarded as a worker or employee, then the client could be liable to pay employment tax and social security on the payments to the contractor, whereas if the contractor works through a personal services company, the client would not currently be liable to pay employment tax or social security on the payments to the personal services company. However, new rules will be introduced from April 2021 under which the client will be liable to pay employment tax and social security on these payments if the working relationship with the contractor is such that, were it not for the personal services company, the contractor would be an employee or worker of the company.

8.2.2. Creating the Relationship

There is no legal requirement for a written contract (commonly referred to as a contract for services) between an independent contractor and the organization they are providing their services to, but in practice there usually will be a contract, and it is helpful to have one. The contract would be taken into account when deciding whether the individual is self-employed, but it is what happens in practice which is most relevant and if the contract does not reflect reality it would be disregarded by the Employment Tribunal.

Unlike England and Wales, workers in Northern Ireland are entitled to written terms of work two months from commencing work however best practice is to issue these as soon as possible. Refer section 2 for more information on what should be included in this statement of particulars.

8.2.3. Compensation

The contract will govern how much the contractor is to be paid for their services. Typically they would receive a day rate, and be expected to provide services for a certain number of days per month. Alternatively they may be paid a project rate, payable in instalments when certain stages of the project are completed.

Self-employed contractors do not benefit from employment rights, apart from protection from discrimination. If the contractor was discriminated against by the client organization, then they may have a claim for compensation (*see* section 17 below).

8.2.4. Other Terms and Conditions

As well as setting out payment terms, an agreement between an organization and a self-employed contractor would typically also include:

- a description of the services to be provided by the contractor;
- whether the services can be subcontracted;
- a warranty that the independent contractor has appropriate insurances;
- notice provisions;
- confidentiality;
- a tax indemnity in favour of the organization in the event that the organization is ordered to pay employment taxes and social security.

8.3. Contract Workers

Contract employees are those who work for a fixed term. They are employees with employment contracts and the same employment rights as permanent employees. Fixed-term employees cannot be treated less favourably than permanent employees, and after four years of successive fixed-term contracts, they automatically become permanent employees.

Temporary workers are individuals who work on assignments, which may be long or short term. Workers are individuals who do not meet the test for employment but are not self-employed either. The statutory definition of a worker is someone who has a contract to do work personally for an organization which is not 'a client or customer of any profession or business undertaking carried on by the individual'.

Workers benefit from some employment protections, including holiday, working time rights (including in relation to working hours and rest breaks), SSP, national minimum wage (NMW), and protection from discrimination. However, workers do not have unfair dismissal protection. Workers are entitled to written terms of work from the first day of work, which must include certain information including details of pay, notice, holiday, sick pay and any benefits (*see* section 2 above).

In Northern Ireland workers are entitled to written terms of work two months from commencing work however best practice is to issue these as soon as possible.

8.4. Leased Workers

A leased worker is not a term commonly used in English employment law. The nearest concept may be that of an agency worker. Agency workers are supplied by an employment agency to a client.

Agency workers are often used:

- to cover for staff shortages caused by illness, holidays, sabbaticals or maternity leave;
- in industries, such as construction, to meet fluctuating demands; or
- to provide cover in unforeseen circumstances, for example, caregivers, nannies and clerical staff.

Agency workers will be employed or engaged by the agency and would not usually have employment rights in relation to the end user client, although there are some exceptions, including discrimination.

The Agency Workers Regulations (AWR) 2010 provides that all agency workers must be able to access a hirer's collective facilities and amenities and have access to information about its job vacancies from the first day of their assignment. In addition, after completion of a twelve-week qualifying period, agency workers are entitled to the same basic working and employment conditions as comparable employees of the end user client.

In Northern Ireland the applicable legislation is the AWR (Northern Ireland) 2011.

An end user would not normally pay the agency worker directly; it is more common to pay the agency, and the agency pays the employee. The benefit of using agency workers is that an end user can stop using them with little or no notice, depending on their terms with the agency.

8.5. Checklist of Dos and Don'ts

- Ensure that a written contract is drafted which clearly defines the relationship between the parties.
- If engaging a contractor, ensure that the relationship is one of self-employment and that the ongoing arrangements are consistent with this, for example, using independent contractors for specific projects or as cover for fixed periods, avoiding integration into the workforce and minimizing control.
- If engaging a worker ensure there is a written statement of work given to the worker on the first day containing minimum information.
- Ensure that certain terms for agency workers are comparable with those of direct employees.

9. OBLIGATION TO BARGAIN COLLECTIVELY WITH TRADE UNIONS: EMPLOYEES' RIGHT TO STRIKE AND A COMPANY'S RIGHT TO CONTINUE BUSINESS OPERATIONS

9.1. Overview of Unions' Rights to Organize

A trade union is a membership organization whose members are mainly workers and whose main purpose includes regulating relations between workers and their employers. A trade union's main aim is usually to protect and advance the interests of its members in the workplace. It does this by offering legal and financial advice to members, discussing members' concerns with their employer, representing members in discussions with the employer about changes to the workplace (e.g., restructures and redundancies) and, in some cases, negotiating with employers about members' pay and working conditions.

Workers are free to create a trade union and trade unions are generally free to seek to encourage workers to join. However, trade unions have no particular rights to represent or negotiate on behalf of workers unless the worker's employer recognizes the union for collective bargaining purposes (*see* below).

The key piece of legislation governing trade unions, their relations with employers and industrial action is the Trade Union and Labour Relations (Consolidation) Act 1992 (TULRCA) in GB, and the Trade Union and Labour Relations (Northern Ireland) Order 1995 in Northern Ireland.

9.2. Right of Employees to Join Unions

Employees have the right to join a union, or multiple unions, of their choice. Employees also have the right not to join a union. Employers must not refuse employment to someone or dismiss an employee because they are, or are not, a member of a union. It is also unlawful to compile, use, sell or supply a 'blacklist' of union members, i.e., a list that will be used to discriminate against them. In addition, employees have the right not to suffer any other unfavourable treatment from their employer for joining or leaving a union or taking part in union activities.

Once an employee is a member of a union, the employer must allow that employee to bring a trade union representative or official as a companion to any formal disciplinary or grievance meeting, including appeal meetings. However, unless the trade union is recognized by the employer for collective bargaining purposes, the union has no special right to represent or negotiate on behalf of an employee in discussions with the employer.

9.3. How Employees Select Unions

Different unions typically represent employees in different sectors, although there are some unions which overlap. In deciding to join a trade union, an employee will typically be guided by factors such as which trade unions are active in their sector, whether their employer recognizes a particular trade union and whether their colleagues are members of a particular union (the more colleagues who are members, the greater influence the union will have).

Union Recognition by Employer

Not all employers in the United Kingdom recognize a trade union for collective bargaining purposes. Trade union recognition is common in sectors such as education, public services, manufacturing, transport and the performing arts. However, it is relatively uncommon in other sectors.

It is possible for an employer and a trade union to agree recognition on a completely voluntary basis, and this is the case for the vast majority of employers who recognize a union. The terms of the recognition and the basis on which the parties will negotiate is recorded in a written agreement, called a recognition agreement or collective bargaining agreement.

If an agreement cannot be reached voluntarily, there is a statutory process by which a trade union can apply for compulsory recognition. The employer (taken together with associated employers incorporated in GB) must have twenty-one or more employees for the application to progress. The union must first submit a request to the employer for recognition. If no agreement is reached, the union must apply to the Central Arbitration Committee (CAC), an independent body established to resolve collective disputes involving trade unions. The union's application must specify a 'bargaining unit' – in effect, the constituency of employees who would be covered by the recognition agreement. This can be the whole workforce, a part of it or a category of workers. The union's application will be inadmissible if the employer already recognizes another trade union for any workers in the proposed bargaining unit.

For the union's application to be admissible, the CAC must be satisfied that at least 10% of the workers in the bargaining unit are members of the union and a majority of workers in the bargaining unit would be likely to be in favour of the union conducting collective bargaining on their behalf. The CAC must then determine whether there is sufficient support for recognition. If the majority of the bargaining unit are union members, the CAC will usually order recognition. If not, the CAC will order a secret ballot of the members of the bargaining unit. Recognition will be granted if a majority of those voting and at least 40% of the bargaining unit vote in favour of recognition.

Once the union is recognized, it will have the right to negotiate with the employer on behalf of workers who are in the bargaining unit over matters such as pay, hours and holidays. This is known as collective bargaining.

Trade unions which are recognized by an employer have a number of other rights including the right to:

- receive information from the employer for collective bargaining purposes;
- be informed and consulted about collective redundancies (*see* section 6.2 above);
- be informed and consulted about business transfers under the Transfer of Undertakings (Protection of Employment) Regulations 2006 (*see* section 7.1 above);
- be informed and consulted about certain changes to pension schemes;
- reasonable paid time off for union officials for union duties or training; and
- reasonable unpaid time off for union members for union activities (such as meetings).

Where a trade union is recognized or seeking to be recognized, it is unlawful for an employer to make an offer directly to any member of the union which, if accepted, would mean any of their terms and conditions of employment would not, or would no longer, be governed by collective bargaining. The penalty for such an unlawful inducement is a mandatory award of GBP 4,341 for each affected employee.

Northern Ireland

The process for a union acquiring recognition, if no agreement is reached, is broadly comparable to that in GB. However, applications in Northern Ireland are made to the Industrial Court. If no agreement is reached, the union may apply to the Industrial Court to decide whether the proposed bargaining unit is appropriate and whether the union has the support from the majority of the workers constituting the appropriate bargaining unit. For the union's application to be admissible the Industrial Court must be satisfied that at least 10% of the workers in the bargaining unit are members of the union. The penalty for unlawful inducement to vote a particular way is a mandatory award of GBP 4,552 for each affected employee.

Right to Strike

A strike constitutes a breach of contract by employees. Action short of strike will often amount to a breach of contract as well. A trade union organizing the strike or industrial action will usually commit the tort of inducing breach of contract (and may commit other torts such as interference with business by unlawful means, intimidation and conspiracy). However, if the trade union satisfies a number of legal requirements when organizing industrial action, the action will be considered 'lawful' or 'protected', meaning the union will be protected from being sued by the employer and employees will be protected from being dismissed for taking part in the action.

The procedures with which a union would need to comply in order to organize lawful or protected industrial action are complex. They are set out in Part V of TULRCA. There have been a number of cases where injunctive action has been used to prevent the industrial action on the basis that an invalid process has been followed (although recent case law suggests that minor discrepancies will no longer be considered sufficient to prevent industrial action taking place). The requirements are explored in outline below. In order for the industrial action to be 'protected' the following conditions must be satisfied:

- The action must be in contemplation or furtherance of a 'trade dispute', i.e., a dispute between workers and their employer which relates wholly or mainly to: terms and conditions of employment; physical working conditions; the allocation of work or duties; matters of discipline; trade union membership; facilities for union officials; the engagement, termination or suspension of workers; or the negotiation or consultation procedures relating to any of the above.
- The union must hold a secret postal ballot which meets certain statutory conditions. The union must give the employer at least fourteen days' notice of the ballot and a copy of the voting papers at least three days' before the ballot.
- The union must also notify the employer of the outcome of the ballot as soon as reasonably practicable.
- The majority of those voting must support the industrial action and at least 50% of all eligible members must have voted.
- The union must also give the employer at least fourteen days' notice of the industrial action, and the action must begin within six months of the ballot (although the parties can agree to extend this up to nine months).

The employer can choose to withhold pay from employees taking part in industrial action (whether or not the action is lawful or protected). However, any dismissal of an employee taking part in protected industrial action will be automatically unfair (there is a limited ability to dismiss fairly if the action continues beyond twelve weeks). The rules on dismissing employees when the industrial action is not protected are complex – in some cases the employer will need to ensure it dismisses all employees as it may face unfair dismissal claims where it dismisses selectively.

If the industrial action is unlawful or unprotected, the employer can seek an injunction to prevent it from happening or seek damages from the union if it goes ahead.

In Northern Ireland the procedures with which a union would need to comply in order to organize lawful or protected industrial action are set out in Part VIII of the Trade Union and Labour Relations (Northern Ireland) Order 1995.

Company's Right to Continue Business Operations

An employer has the right to continue its business operations during a strike or other industrial action. The employer can use existing employees from other parts of the business or hire employees on fixed-term contracts to cover the work of striking employees. However, it is a criminal offence for an employment business to supply agency workers to cover the work of striking employees or the work of other employees who have been reassigned to cover striking employees. An employer that so engages agency workers would likely be liable for aiding and abetting the commission of that offence. The penalty is an unlimited fine.

9.4. Pre-election Campaigning

Employers have a duty under TULRCA to cooperate with trade unions and ballot supervisors in connection with a recognition ballot, and also to allow unions reasonable access to employees prior to the ballot. There is a statutory Code of Practice on Access and Unfair Practices during Recognition and Derecognition Ballots (AURD Code) which sets out guidelines for employers and trade unions in relation to campaigns and communications around recognition and derecognition ballots. The Code makes recommendations for how unions might have access to employees for campaigning, and encourages employers and trade unions to enter into an access agreement.

9.5. Unfair Labour Practices

Balloting for Trade Union Recognition

Both employers and trade unions have a statutory duty to refrain from using unfair practices in connection with a ballot. Examples of practices which would be unfair, and therefore unlawful, include bribing or coercing an employee to vote in a particular way, or threatening to discipline or dismiss an employee in connection with the ballot. The AURD Code gives further detail on what might be regarded as an unfair practice, and makes recommendations for measures to ensure transparency and good practice in campaigning.

9.6. Relocation of Work/Shutdown of Business

Employers proposing to relocate or close down a business will need to consider any provisions under any collective agreement with a trade union which may require them to consult with the union in relation to these types of proposals. In addition, employers will need to consider individual redundancy consultation, and possibly collective consultation, depending on the number of employees affected.

Employers may also have an employee consultation body in place, which the employers are required to consult with on such matters. Employee consultation bodies may be set up by agreement, or by the statutory procedure under the Information and Consultation of Employees Regulations 2005 which govern the process for setting up a national works council.

9.7. Checklist of Dos and Don'ts

- Do not refuse employment to anyone or dismiss an employee because they are or are not a member of a trade union.
- Do not treat an employee unfavourably for joining or leaving a union or taking part in union activities.
- Where a trade union is seeking recognition, and has majority support from workers, do consider entering into a collective bargaining agreement on a voluntary basis (rather than risk having a compulsory recognition agreement imposed).
- Where a trade union is recognized or seeking recognition, do not make any offers direct to union members which would have the effect of inducing them to opt out of collective bargaining.
- Do ensure that any strike or industrial action organized by a trade union is supported by a lawful ballot that satisfies the statutory criteria and that the union has complied with its notice obligations in relation to the strike.
- Do not engage agency workers to cover the work of striking employees or of other employees reassigned to cover the work of striking employees.

10. WORKING CONDITIONS: HOURS OF WORK AND PAYMENT OF WAGES: BY STATUTE OR COLLECTIVE AGREEMENTS

10.1. Overview of Wage and Hour Laws

The key rules relating to hours of work in the UK are set out in the Working Time Regulations (WTR) 1998. The WTR impose rules on the maximum number of hours in the working week; the number and length of rest breaks in the working week; and the minimum amount of paid annual leave.

The key rules relating to wages are set out in the NMW Act 1998 and the associated National Minimum Wage Regulations 2015 (NMW Regulations). The NMW Act and NMW Regulations provide for a minimum wage to be paid to all UK workers.

The ERA 1996 also contains further protections for workers' wages, including the right not to suffer unauthorized deductions from wages.

10.2. Minimum Wage

All employers in the UK are obliged to pay their workers a prescribed minimum hourly rate of pay. This is known as the NMW.

A worker is an individual who works under a contract of employment or a contract (express or implied) to personally do or perform work or services for another, provided that the other is not a customer or client of a profession or business undertaking carried on by the individual. This is intended to exclude those who are genuinely self-employed.

There are five different rates of NMW for different age-related categories of worker:

- National Living Wage: for workers aged 23 and over (there is no upper age limit).
- Standard (adult) rate: for workers aged between 21 and 22 inclusive.
- Development rate: for workers aged between 18 and 20 inclusive.
- Young workers rate: for workers aged under 18 but over 16 (the compulsory school age) that are not apprentices.
- Apprenticeship rate: for apprentices under 19 or in the first year of their apprenticeship.

As of 1 April 2021, the rates were GBP 8.91, GBP 8.36, GBP 6.56, GBP 4.62 and GBP 4.30 respectively per hour (the rates increase annually every April).

The policy behind the NMW is that workers should receive the NMW in the form of cash rather than benefits in kind. The only non-cash benefit that may be taken into account is the value of any accommodation provided by the employer to the worker, up to a set allowance.

The NMW is assessed by reference to a worker's hourly rate of pay over a 'pay reference period'. The pay reference period is one month or, if the worker is paid by reference to a period shorter than a month, the worker's actual pay period.

The employer must ensure that the worker receives the NMW in each pay reference period. A failure to do so would entitle the worker to bring a claim for unlawful deductions from wages (*see* below) or breach of contract. The employer may also be exposed to other enforcement action by Her Majesty's Revenue and Customs (HMRC) such as civil penalties, recovery of underpayments, 'naming and shaming' and criminal prosecution. It is an offence for an employer to refuse or wilfully neglect to pay the NMW, punishable with a potentially unlimited fine.

10.3. Overtime

There is no specific law governing overtime in the UK. Whether workers may be required to work overtime is a matter for agreement between the worker and their employer. Employment contracts, collective agreements or employer's policies may provide for an enhanced rate of pay for overtime, but this is not obligatory.

The WTR impose a restriction on the maximum number of hours that can be worked each week. A worker's average working time (including overtime) must not exceed forty-eight hours per week. Overtime for these purposes includes any work outside normal working hours, whether or not it forms part of a contractual right. Employers must take all reasonable steps to ensure that this limit is complied with. Failure to do so is an offence punishable with a potentially unlimited fine.

The limit on the length of the working week will not apply to workers who agree to 'opt out' of the limit. To do so, the worker must agree in writing that the forty-eight-hour limit does not apply, and the agreement must be capable of being withdrawn by the worker on giving not more than three months' written notice to the employer. If the opt-out agreement fails to specify a notice period for withdrawal, the worker will be entitled to withdraw the opt-out on giving seven days' prior notice.

The following points should be considered with regard to opt-out agreements:

– Even if a worker has agreed to opt out, the worker cannot be required to work excessively long hours if this creates a reasonably foreseeable risk to the worker's health and safety, or the health and safety of others.

- A worker who opts out will still, in effect, be subject to an average maximum working week of seventy-six hours taking account of the minimum rest break requirements (*see* below).
- A worker cannot be forced to sign an opt-out agreement. Any employer who disadvantages a worker as a result of refusing to sign an opt-out – e.g., through reduced pay and benefits, diminished promotion prospects, dismissal – will be in breach of the WTR.
- Employers must keep records showing which workers have opted out covering at least two years.
- Although it is unlawful to dismiss a worker or otherwise victimize them for refusing to sign an opt-out agreement (or for withdrawing an opt-out agreement), there is currently no prohibition on refusing to employ someone unless they opt out. Some employers include an opt-out in job offer letters or in the contract of employment itself, but this practice has attracted considerable criticism from both unions and employers as being an abuse of the opt-out.

The forty-eight-hour limit does not apply to workers who have 'unmeasured' working time – i.e., where, due to the nature of the worker's role, the duration of working time is not measured or can be determined by the worker, such as a managing executive with autonomous decision-making powers. In addition, there are separate rules for working time in relation to workers in certain industries, such as certain boat crews and fisherman, services within the police and armed forces, and mobile workers in the air and road transport sectors.

The WTR also contain special protections for 'young workers', i.e., anyone over compulsory school age (16 years) but under 18 years. Young workers cannot work more than eight hours a day or forty hours a week, except where their work is necessary in order to maintain continuity of service or production or respond to a surge in demand, and there is no adult who could carry out the work. These limits are absolute – they cannot be averaged nor can the young worker give their consent to opt out.

10.4. Meal and Rest Periods

The WTR prescribe minimum entitlements for three different types of break:

- a twenty-minute 'quick break' if the working day lasts for six hours or more. The 'quick break' must be uninterrupted (e.g., four breaks of five minutes will not suffice) and must be taken during the working day (i.e., not tacked on to the end of the day). A daily lunch break would count as a 'quick break';

- an eleven-hour uninterrupted 'daily rest break', once every twenty-four hours;
- a twenty-four-hour uninterrupted 'weekly rest break' once every seven days. Time off at weekends would count as a worker's weekly rest break. Further, additional flexibility in the WTR allows employers to give workers one uninterrupted forty-eight-hour rest break once every fourteen days, or two uninterrupted twenty-four-hour rest breaks twice during any fourteen-day period (instead of twenty-four hours in each seven-day period).

The WTR do not make any provision regarding pay for such breaks but workers may have rights to pay under their employment contracts or in a collective agreement (e.g., paid lunch breaks). Employers are not expected to force workers to take their breaks but should ensure that they have a proper opportunity to do so, e.g., by arranging working patterns in a way that enables workers to take the required breaks.

An employer can, through a collective agreement or workforce agreement, vary the rest breaks outlined above. However, the employer would have to provide other rest breaks to workers as compensation and such breaks would need to be at least as long.

Young workers (*see* above) have an enhanced entitlement to breaks. Young workers are entitled to a thirty-minute 'quick break' if the working day last for four and a half hours or more; a twelve-hour uninterrupted 'daily rest break' once every twenty-four hours; and a forty-eight-hour uninterrupted 'weekly rest break' once every seven days. There is no entitlement to pay for these breaks under the WTR.

10.5. Deductions from Wages

The ERA provides the right for all workers not to have unauthorized deductions made from their wages. The basic position is that it is unlawful for an employer to make a deduction from a worker's wages unless:

- the deduction is required or authorized by statute or a provision in the worker's contract; or
- the worker has given their prior written consent to the deduction.

Certain deductions are required or authorized by statutes, such as deductions for income tax and national insurance (social security) contributions or deductions to reimburse the employer for the overpayment of wages.

If the deduction is made under a provision of the worker's contract, then the worker must have seen the term or (if it is not a written contract) must have been told in writing of its effect before the deduction is made. The contractual provision and the worker's prior written consent need to make it clear that the deduction will be made from the worker's wages. The employer must also demonstrate that the event justifying the deduction has occurred.

A worker whose employer has made an unlawful deduction from their wages can bring a claim in an Employment Tribunal to recover the amount of the deduction. Such claims must be brought within three months of the deduction or, where there is a series of deductions, within three months of the last in the series. Most claims for unlawful deductions can only go back as far as the last two years, even where there is a series of deductions.

Northern Ireland

As noted in section 11 below, the WTR (Northern Ireland) 2016 are the applicable regulations in Northern Ireland and employers in Northern Ireland should be mindful of recent case law in relation to the calculation of holiday pay, namely *Chief Constable for the Police Service of Northern Ireland Policy Board v. Alexander Agnew and Others* [NICA] 2019. The Northern Ireland Court of Appeal has ruled that workers can make claims back to 1998 (when the WTR (Northern Ireland) 1998 were introduced) for any alleged unlawful deductions made in relation to holiday pay; i.e., there should not be a two-year backstop. The Police Service of Northern Ireland has been granted leave from the Supreme Court to appeal this decision.

10.6. Garnishment

The Attachment of Earnings Act 1971 enables courts to make an attachment of earnings order. An attachment of earnings order is an order that compels an employer to make regular deductions from an employee's earnings and pay them to the court where a court judgment has been made against the employee. An application for an attachment of earnings order will only be successful if all the following conditions are met:

- A court judgment has been made against the employee to pay a sum of money.
- The employee is behind with at least one payment towards the judgment debt.
- The amount remaining due under the judgment is at least GBP 50.
- The individual is employed (an order cannot be made if the individual is self-employed or unemployed).
- It is made within six years of the judgment becoming enforceable.

The Attachment of Earnings Act 1971 does not extend to Scotland or Northern Ireland. The equivalent under Scots law is an earnings arrestment under the Debtors (Scotland) Act 1987. In Northern Ireland, the Judgements Enforcement (Northern Ireland) Order 1981 enables courts to make an attachment of earnings order.

10.7. Exemptions to Wage and Hour Laws

The WTR do not apply at all to certain boat crews and fishermen. Also, the provisions dealing with maximum weekly working time, night work and rest breaks do not apply to services within the police and armed forces, or mobile workers in the air and road transport sectors. Separate rules apply to these workers. In addition, the WTR allow employers to adapt and/or exclude certain provisions by agreement with workers and/or their representatives.

There are comparatively few exemptions to the NMW Act and NMW Regulations (e.g., domestic workers who are treated as part of the family for whom they work and persons volunteering for a charity are exempt from the NMW).

10.8. Child Labour

The Children and Young Persons Act (CYPA) 1933 sets out minimum age requirements, restrictions on the hours that children can work and the type of work in which they can be involved. Any person who is not over compulsory school age (16 years) is deemed to be a child for these purposes. The Education Act 1996 (EA96) also contains rules for children who are on work experience placements as part of their education. There are also separate rules regarding public performances by children.

In addition to these statutory restrictions, local authorities can make bye-laws regulating the employment of children. These bye-laws can impose further restrictions on the nature and hours of work children can do. Many bye-laws, for example, require children to have a permit to undertake work. Employers should therefore always check the bye-laws with the relevant local authority before employing children.

Generally speaking, it is unlawful to employ children below the age of 14 years. However, some local authority bye-laws permit 13-year-old children to be employed in certain roles, e.g., delivering newspapers or stacking shelves. Under the CYPA 1933, children may only be employed to do 'light work', i.e., work that is unlikely to be harmful to their safety, health, development, school attendance or participation in work experience.

Children cannot be employed in street trading unless permitted by a local authority bye-law.

There are also restrictions on the hours that children can work under CYPA 1933. Generally, children cannot be employed before 7 am or after 7 pm or for more than two hours on a school day or Sunday, or for more than twelve hours in any week during the school term. Further, children cannot be employed for more than eight hours a day (if aged 15 or over) or five hours a day (if under 15) even on a non-school day (other than Sunday where the limit is two hours). During school holidays, children can work up to thirty-five hours a week (if aged 15 or over) or twenty-five hours a week (if under 15). Children must have a one-hour rest break after working four hours in any day and must be given a two-week break from any employment in each year. As set out above, these restrictions are subject to any further restrictions set out in a relevant bye-law.

The CYPA 1933 and EA96 do not extend to Scotland, but there are broadly equivalent provisions under the Children and Young Persons (Scotland) Act 1937 and the Education (Scotland) Act 1980. In Northern Ireland, the applicable legislation is the CYPA (Northern Ireland) 1968 and the Education (Northern Ireland) Order 1997.

In addition to these restrictions for children, the WTR impose additional protections for 'young workers', i.e., anyone over compulsory school age (16 years) but under 18 years. These include limits on weekly working hours and entitlement to particular rest breaks (*see* above).

10.9. Recordkeeping Requirements

Both the WTR and the NMW Regulations require employers to keep records.

10.9.1. Information That Must Be Maintained

Apart from the recordkeeping obligations outlined below, there are no general rules relating to specific information that must be maintained by employers.

10.9.2. Records That Must Be Retained

Under the WTR, employers must keep records to show that the forty-eight-hour maximum working week, the restrictions on night work and the restrictions in relation to young workers have been complied with. In practice, this means keeping a record of workers' working hours. However, employers do not need to keep records of working hours for those who have 'unmeasured' working time or those who have opted out of the forty-eight-hour working week (other than a record of the opt-out itself). Records must be kept for two years.

Under the NMW Regulations, employers will also need to keep pay and time records for workers sufficient to demonstrate that workers have received the NMW. The exact information required will depend on the circumstances, including how workers are paid and what deductions are made from their pay. Such records must be made available for inspection by workers or HMRC enforcement officers. Records must be kept for a minimum of six years from the end of the pay reference period to which they relate.

10.9.3. Failure to Maintain Required Records

Employers who fail to comply with the recordkeeping obligations under the WTR or the NMW Regulations will be guilty of an offence punishable by a potentially unlimited fine. The Health and Safety Executive (HSE) has overall responsibility for enforcing the WTR, whereas HMRC is responsible for enforcing the NMW Act and NMW Regulations.

In Northern Ireland, the HSE of Northern Ireland has the responsibility of enforcing the WTR (Northern Ireland) 2016.

10.10. Reductions in Compensation Caused by Economic Downturn

A reduction in salary or change in contractual benefits for any reason, including an economic downturn, will constitute a change to the employee's terms and conditions of employment. Employers will therefore generally need the employee's consent for such a contractual variation. Employees are sometimes more willing to agree with such changes in an economic downturn, particularly where they would otherwise face the prospect of potential redundancies.

An employer wishing to reduce an employee's salary or contractual benefits without consent would be acting in breach of contract (unless there is a specific clause in the contract of employment permitting such reduction, which is rare – a general clause allowing an employer the flexibility to change a contract of employment is unlikely to be sufficient). Employees in these circumstances have the option to resign and claim constructive unfair dismissal or to continue working 'under protest' while reserving the right to sue for any loss suffered. To avoid this, the employer could terminate the employment contract on notice and offer a new contract on the revised salary. This is known as 'termination and re-engagement' or 'fire and rehire'. The termination would be a dismissal and any employee with at least two years' service could bring an unfair dismissal claim. However, the employer may be able to defend such a claim if it can show that it had a sound business reason for the change and that it acted reasonably in introducing the change. In practice, this will mean showing that the employer has consulted with staff and tried to get their agreement to the change.

In Northern Ireland, employees only need one year's service to bring an unfair dismissal claim.

Where changes to the salary of twenty or more employees are involved, this is likely to trigger the duty to consult collectively (*see* section 6 above). This would certainly be the case if the employer proposed to dismiss twenty or more employees and offer re-engagement on revised terms, or where the salary reduction is such that twenty or more employees could resign and claim constructive unfair dismissal.

10.11. Checklist of Dos and Don'ts

- Ensure that workers do not work beyond the forty-eight-hour maximum weekly working limit or workers are asked to sign an agreement to opt out of the forty-eight-hour limit.
- Ensure that working time is structured so that workers are able to take their required rest breaks, including daily and weekly rest breaks.
- Ensure all workers receive at least the NMW for the hours they work, averaged over the relevant pay reference period.
- Keep adequate records to demonstrate compliance with the limits on working hours and that workers have received the NMW.
- Where changes to salary or benefits are proposed (whether in an economic downturn or otherwise), consult with staff and try to reach their agreement before implementing the change.

11. OTHER WORKING CONDITIONS AND BENEFITS: BY STATUTE, COLLECTIVE AGREEMENTS, OR COMPANY POLICY

11.1. Health and Other Insurance

There is no obligation on UK employers to provide health or other insurance benefits to employees, although many employers choose to offer these benefits.

11.2. Pension and Retirement Benefits

UK employees are eligible for two types of pension – a state pension and an employer pension.

State Pensions

Employees are eligible to receive a state pension at state pension age, provided they have paid national insurance contributions (which are deducted from salary along with income tax) for a sufficient number of years. The state pension age is currently 66. It will increase to 67 in 2028, and eventually will increase to 68 (on a date yet to be set).

The weekly rate of the state pension is currently GBP 179.60 (for employees who paid national insurance contributions for 35 years, with lower rates applying to who paid contributions for fewer years). The rate increases annually every April.

Auto-Enrolment

Employers are required to enrol their workers who are aged at least 22 and earning at least GBP 10,000 per year, in a pension scheme meeting certain minimum requirements, usually within six weeks of the worker starting work.

The pension scheme may be a scheme that is operated by the employer or by a third party pension provider, as long as it meets the minimum requirements, or the employer may choose to use a Government operated scheme known as NEST.

The total contribution made into the scheme on behalf of the worker must be at least 8% (this contribution is paid on the worker's annual earnings between GBP 6,240 and GBP 50,270). The employer must contribute at least 3%, and if it only contributed this minimum amount, the worker would then be required to contribute 5% to make up the 8% in total.

Workers can opt out of the pension scheme if they wish, but if they do the employer must re-enrol them again every three years (and each time they may opt out again if they choose).

11.3. Vacation and Holiday Payments on Termination

All workers are entitled to a minimum of 5.6 weeks' paid holiday per year (which amounts to twenty-eight days' holiday for a full-time worker). There are eight public holidays in the UK which may be included within the paid holiday which the worker is entitled to take. Some employers offer more than the minimum amount, for example, twenty-five days plus the eight public holidays.

Holiday pay should be worker's usual rate of pay, including overtime and allowances (such as shift allowances). If the worker has variable hours or variable pay, so that pay differs from one week or month to the next, then holiday pay must be calculated using an average of pay over the previous fifty-two weeks.

Workers may carry over up to 1.6 weeks of their holiday entitlement to be used in the following holiday year. On termination of employment, a worker is entitled to pay in lieu of unused annual leave.

Northern Ireland

In Northern Ireland there are ten bank and public holidays which may be included within the paid holiday which the worker is entitled to take. In relation to the calculation of holiday pay, statute provides that this should be based on the average rate of remuneration payable to the employee in the previous twelve weeks. However, the case of *Chief Constable for the Police Service of Northern Ireland Policy Board v. Alexander Agnew and Others* [NICA] 2019 has resulted in many uncertainties with regard to calculating holiday pay. The Police Service of Northern Ireland has been granted leave to appeal this decision to the Supreme Court; however, in summary, the three most significant directions given by the Northern Ireland Court of Appeal in relation to calculating holiday pay are:

(1) workers in Northern Ireland are entitled to pursue claims for a shortfall in holiday pay from the date of commencement of the WTR (Northern Ireland) 1998;
(2) workers are entitled to annual leave from whichever source (e.g., the WTR (Northern Ireland) 1998), contract or otherwise; there is no requirement for certain types of leave to be taken in any particular order; and

(3) for employees whose pay varies, the appropriate reference period to calculate holiday pay is fact sensitive to each case and should be based on the number of days actually worked in the previous year.

11.4. LEAVES OF ABSENCE

11.4.1. Personal Leave

There is no concept of 'personal leave' in the UK. However, employees may take sick leave, family leave such as maternity, paternity and parental leave (*see* below).

Employees have a right to take reasonable time off to deal with emergencies involving dependants. A dependant includes a child, partner and parent, and the time off may be taken to provide assistance when a dependant is ill, to arrange emergency care for a dependant, or in connection with the death of a dependant. This time off is unpaid.

11.4.2. Medical or Sick Leave

Workers may be absent from work due to illness. They may be entitled to SSP, depending on the length of the illness. The rules governing SSP are complex but broadly workers who are unable to work due to illness for at least four days may be eligible for SSP, for up to twenty-eight weeks. The weekly rate of SSP is currently GBP 96.35 (and increases annually each April).

Some employers provide contractual sick pay as well as SSP, but there is no obligation to do so. If this is offered, it will usually be for a limited number of weeks in any rolling twelve-month period.

Some employers provide employees with a membership of a permanent health insurance plan, which will provide payment of salary (typically 60%–75% of salary) where an employee is absent due to long-term sickness (policies pay out typically after six months of absence).

11.4.3. Bereavement Leave

In April 2020 a new right to parental bereavement leave was introduced (although *see* below in relation to Northern Ireland). A parent who loses a child under the age of 18, or whose baby is stillborn after twenty-four weeks of pregnancy, may take up to two weeks' leave. This leave will be paid at the statutory rate, currently GBP 151.97 (increasing annually each April), or 90% of pay if this is lower than GBP 151.97.

As of April 2021, bereavement leave has not come into force in Northern Ireland. UK Government guidance suggests that if an employee lives in Northern Ireland and is employed by a company in GB under a contract of employment in accordance with the ERA 1996, the employee will be eligible for statutory bereavement leave. However, if an employee lives in Northern Ireland and is employed under a contract of employment made in accordance with the Employment Rights (Northern Ireland) Order 1996, they will not qualify for statutory parental bereavement leave.

There is no statutory right to take bereavement leave in respect of other family or friends, although many employers choose to offer a period of time off, either paid or unpaid, to employees who are bereaved.

11.4.4. Family Leave

There is no concept of 'family leave' in UK law but there are different types of leave and time off which may be taken in connection with pregnancy, children and family. These are:

- Time off for antenatal care/adoption appointments.
- Maternity leave.
- Adoption leave.
- Paternity leave.
- Shared parental leave.
- Parental leave.

These are all described in more detail below.

11.4.5. Pregnancy Leave

All pregnant employees have a statutory right to reasonable paid time off for antenatal care, regardless of hours worked or length of service. As well as medical appointments, antenatal care could include relaxation classes and parentcraft classes, provided that these are advised by a registered medical practitioner, midwife or health visitor. The child's father or mother's partner may take unpaid leave to attend up to two antenatal appointments with the mother.

An employee who is the primary adopter of a child may take paid time off to attend up to five adoption appointments, and their partner may take unpaid leave to attend two appointments (if the parents are joint adopters they may decide between them which is the primary adopter for the purposes of time off to attend adoption appointments).

11.4.6. Maternity Leave

Maternity leave is one of a number of different types of leave available to parents. The other types of leave are adoption leave, paternity leave, shared parental leave and parental leave. The amounts of statutory leave and pay available are set out below, although many employers choose to enhance the statutory pay for family leave (e.g., paying full salary for the first thirteen weeks of maternity leave and half salary for the next thirteen weeks).

Maternity Leave

All pregnant employees, regardless of the length of service, are entitled to fifty-two weeks of statutory maternity leave.

If the employee satisfies minimum earnings criteria and has twenty-six weeks' continuous employment at the end of the fifteenth week before the week that the baby is due, she may be eligible for statutory maternity pay (SMP). SMP is paid at 90% of normal earnings for the first six weeks, and then at the statutory flat rate for the next thirty-three weeks (or 90% of earnings if this is less than the statutory rate). The statutory rate is currently GBP 151.97, and increases annually each April. The last thirteen weeks of the fifty-two-week maternity leave period are unpaid.

Employees may be made redundant while on maternity leave (as long as the redundancy is unconnected with the pregnancy or maternity leave), but if there is any suitable alternative employment available the employee on maternity leave must be offered this (in priority to other redundant employees).

The employee's partner may take paternity leave (*see* below).

Adoption Leave

An employee who is adopting a child is entitled to take up to fifty-two weeks' adoption leave, regardless of their length of service. The employee will be entitled to statutory adoption pay, if they satisfy minimum earnings criteria and have at least twenty-six weeks' service at the date they are matched with a child for adoption. Statutory adoption pay is paid at the same rate as SMP, and the same rights in relation to returning to work and redundancy apply.

The employee's partner may take paternity leave (*see* below).

Paternity Leave

The child's father (or if the parents are not together, the mother's/adopter's partner) is entitled to take up to two weeks' paternity leave. Paternity leave must be taken within fifty-six days of the child's birth/adoption. If the employee meets minimum earnings criteria and has at least twenty-six weeks' service at the fifteenth week before the week the child is due/matched for adoption, they will be entitled to statutory paternity pay. Statutory paternity pay is currently paid at a weekly rate of GBP 151.97 (which increases annually each April) or 90% of earnings if this is less then GBP 151.97.

Shared Parental Leave

An employee may give up part of their maternity or adoption leave, in order for the employee and or the child's father/employee's partner to take this leave as shared parental leave. The parents can choose between them how this is taken and may take it in turns or at the same time, as long as it is taken within one year of the child's birth/adoption. If the mother gives up any of the paid part of maternity/adoption leave, then this statutory pay will be available to be used during shared parental leave.

Parental Leave

An employee may take parental leave in respect of a child up to the age of 18 (although similarly named this is different from the shared parental leave referred to above). The entitlement is a total of eighteen weeks per child, and up to four weeks per child may be taken in any one year. Parental leave is unpaid.

11.4.7. Injury at Work

Time off due to injury at work is likely to be covered by an employer's normal rules on sickness absence. An employee who is injured at work may have a personal injury claim against the employer, which may be covered by the employer's insurance.

11.5. Checklist of Dos and Don'ts

Set out in a relevant policy, the circumstances when an employee is entitled to be paid for time taken off work.

If insurances are to be provided as a benefit, ensure that entitlement is always subject to the terms of the insurance scheme and ensure that flexibility is maintained to change the insurance provider and/or the scheme/level of cover where necessary.

12. WORKERS' COMPENSATION

12.1. Overview

There are a number of Government schemes to cover certain illnesses/injuries caused by work, including those caused by working with asbestos.

The amounts payable and availability of the schemes depend on the scheme in question and the specified illness/injury. A non-exhaustive list of available schemes is set out below and the latest Government guidance should be referred to before making any claim:

- There is a Government scheme for Industrial Injuries Disablement Benefit (IIDB), covering certain illnesses caused by work, including those caused by working with asbestos. The amounts payable under the scheme depend on the extent of the disability and the weekly payments currently range from GBP 36.58 to GBP 182.90.
- Under the IIDB an individual can also claim the Constant Attendance Allowance where the disability in question is assessed at 100% and you require daily care and attention. The weekly payments currently range from GBP 36.60 to GBP 219.60 (taking into account the Exceptionally Severe Disablement Allowance).
- Individuals may also be eligible for a Reduced Earning Allowance of GBP 73.16 a week for accidents that happened, or diseases that started, before 1 October 1990.
- Certain individuals may also be eligible for a 'lump-sum' payment under the Pneumoconiosis Etc. (Workers' Compensation) Act 1979. Schemes are also run by the Ministry of Defence. Where neither of these is available, an individual still may be able to claim diffuse mesothelioma payments, either under the '2008 scheme' or the Diffuse Mesothelioma Payment Scheme.

12.2. Checklist of Dos and Don'ts

Not applicable. Refer to the latest Government guidance.

13. COMPANY'S OBLIGATION TO PROVIDE SAFE AND HEALTHY WORKPLACE

13.1. Overview of Safety and Environmental Laws and Regulations

Employers have common law and statutory duties relating to the health and safety of their employees, contractors and members of the public.

At common law, an employer must take 'reasonable care' for the health and safety of its employees, contractors and members of the public. This means that employers:

- must provide and maintain a safe place of work, a safe system of work and safe and proper equipment (including plant and machinery);
- must employ competent staff;
- can be vicariously liable for the results of the negligent acts of their employees while working in the course of their employment;
- can be liable for certain occupational diseases (e.g., asbestosis) if they are considered to have been on notice of the risks of the disease materializing;
- can be liable where an injured person can show that an employer or individual had a duty to take reasonable care towards them, and they have suffered the injury through a breach of that duty. The injured person must also show that the type of loss or injury for which damages are being claimed was a foreseeable result of the breach of the duty.

Under the Health and Safety at Work etc. Act 1974 (HSWA 1974), its related regulations and approved codes of practice:

(a) An employer has a general duty 'to ensure, so far as is reasonably practicable, the health, safety and welfare at work of all [its] employees' and those that are otherwise affected by their activities.

(b) In particular, an employer should ensure:
  - it sufficiently and suitably assesses and reviews the work-related risks faced by employees and others affected by their activities;
  - implementation and maintenance of plant and systems of work that are, so far as is reasonably practicable, safe and without risks to health;
  - safe use, handling, storage and transport of articles and substances;
  - provision of information, instruction, training and supervision as is required to ensure, so far as is reasonably practicable, the health and safety of employees at work and auditing the adequacy of these procedures on a regular basis;

- places of work under the employer's control are, so far as is reasonably practicable, safe for work and without risks to health (with safe entrances and exits);
- provision and maintenance of a safe working environment with adequate facilities and arrangements for welfare at work;
- it displays the health and safety law poster (as available on the HSE website) or provides each worker with a copy of the equivalent pocket card.

In Northern Ireland, the Health and Safety at Work (Northern Ireland) Order 1978 is the applicable legislation.

13.2. Requirements

If an employer employs five or more people, it must:

- have a written statement of its general health and safety policy (a health and safety policy statement) with respect to its employees and organization;
- implement arrangements for carrying out the policy, and bring it to the attention of all its employees;
- revise the policy whenever appropriate;
- record any arrangements that are put into place; and
- make a record of the significant findings of risk assessments (e.g., groups of employees identified as being especially at risk).

A written document ensures that both the employer and its workforce are clear about their respective responsibilities. Therefore, although an employer with less than five people in its workforce is not legally obliged to have a written health and safety policy statement, a written policy can improve health and safety within its organization.

Employees also have responsibilities under health and safety legislation to cooperate with their employer so far as is necessary to enable compliance with any statutory duty or requirement relating to health and safety.

Coronavirus Management Requirements

The spread of COVID-19 in 2020 and 2021 has required employers and businesses in the UK to carefully consider the duty of care owed to employees, contractors and customers on-site.

COVID-19 has been added to statute (Infectious Diseases (Amendment) Regulations 2020) and has been declared an infectious disease subject to statutory control as from 28 February 2020. As set out above, employers have common law and statutory duties relating to the health and safety of their employees, contractors and members of the public, which extends to taking steps to contain infectious diseases and prevent the infection of others or the exposure of others to the risk of infection. To discharge these duties businesses must show that they took reasonable steps in mitigating the relevant risks. A starting point for many employers and businesses will be the review and implementation of suitable risk assessment procedures, in line with the recommendations set out in Public Health England's industry-specific 'Working Safely during coronavirus (COVID-19) guidance', which is updated on a regular basis.

All employers must carry out a risk assessment, however employers with fewer than five employees are not required to write anything down (though it is best practice to do so). The risk assessment must:

- identify what work activity or situations might cause transmission of the virus;
- think about who could be at risk;
- decide how likely it is that someone could be exposed;
- act to remove the activity or situation, or if this is not possible, control the risk;
- also consider groups who are more at risk of being infected and/or having an adverse outcome if infected (Public Health England have published a review looking into how different factors affect COVID-19 risk and outcomes which can be accessed here).

The characteristics of differing workplace settings will ultimately guide the requirements for a comprehensive risk assessment, however in general, key steps to be considered include:

- Consultation with workers, trade unions and/or stakeholders.
- Documenting H&S risk assessments (website publication expected for all businesses with over fifty employees).
- Creating or updating H&S policies and procedures.
- Health screening and monitoring.
- Identification of vulnerable and high-risk individuals.
- Provision of suitable personal protective equipment ('PPE') (only where necessary).
- Workload management (resulting from staffing reductions) – of note, mental health is a key area of risk and one specifically flagged by the HSE.
- Modifications to the workplace set-up.

All employers should regularly update their COVID-19 risk assessment to reflect any changes in legislation or guidance. Once a risk assessment has been completed and appropriate measures have been put in place the employer has an ongoing monitoring duty to ensure that the measures put in place are working as expected.

13.3. Rights of Employees

Generally, employees can expect the following with regard to health and safety at work:

- To work in places where, as far as possible, any risks to their health and safety are properly controlled.
- To stop working and leave the working area if they think they are in danger (without being disciplined).
- To inform their employer about health and safety issues or concerns.
- To contact the HSE or their local authority if they still have health and safety concerns (without being disciplined, if the employer does not listen to their concerns).
- Free of charge, to be provided with any equipment and protective clothing that they need and to ensure it is properly looked after.
- To be paid to have time off work for training (if they are a safety representative).

In Northern Ireland, the HSE for Northern Ireland is the relevant governing body where health and safety concerns should be reported.

13.4. Rights of Employer

The employer has obligations, not rights, under health and safety law.

13.5. Specific Standards

The Management of Health and Safety at Work Regulations 1999 (the Management Regulations) generally make more explicit what employers are required to do to manage health and safety under the HSWA 1974. Like the Act, they apply to every work activity. The main requirement of employers is to assess and manage risks to their employees and, where appropriate, others, arising from work activities, including carrying out a risk assessment. Employers with five or more employees need to record the significant findings of the risk assessment in writing.

Risk assessments should be appropriate for the employer's type of work/workplace. Therefore, generally they will be more straightforward in a typical office but will be more involved where it deals with more serious hazards such as those on a power station, manufacturing facility, laboratory or an oil rig.

In Northern Ireland, the Management of Health and Safety at Work Regulations (Northern Ireland) 2000 is the applicable legislation.

13.6. Injury or Accident at Work

An employer has a legal duty under the Reporting of Injuries, Diseases and Dangerous Occurrences Regulations (RIDDOR) 2013 to report certain serious workplace accidents, occupational diseases and specified dangerous occurrences (near misses).

The following types of incidents should be reported to the HSE:

- Deaths and major injuries caused by workplace accidents.
- Specified injuries to workers.
- Injuries to members of the public or people not at work where they are taken from the scene of an accident to the hospital.
- Over-seven-day incapacitation of a worker – accidents must be reported where they result in an employee or self-employed person being away from work, or unable to perform their normal work duties, for more than seven consecutive days as the result of their injury.
- Some occupational/work-related diseases.
- Exposure to carcinogens, mutagens and biological agents (including occupational cancers).
- Dangerous occurrences – where something happens that does not result in an injury but could reasonably have done any serious injury or cause death (which may be specific to the type of industry/workplace involved).
- Gas Safe registered gas fitters must also report dangerous gas fittings they find (to the extent that people could die, be rendered unconscious or need to be taken to hospital), and gas conveyors/suppliers must report some flammable gas incidents.
- Over-three-day injuries – accidents must be recorded, but not reported where they result in a worker being incapacitated for more than three consecutive days.

Employers must keep a record of any reportable injury, disease or dangerous occurrence. This must include the date and method of reporting; the date, time and place of the event; personal details of those involved; and a brief description of the nature of the event or disease. Records can be kept in any of the following formats:

- Keeping paper copies of report forms in a file.
- Recording the details on a computer.

- Using an Accident Book system.
- Maintaining a written log.

A company with more than ten employees must have an accident book. RIDDOR records must be kept for a minimum of three years after the date of the last incident in the book (although best practice is to keep records for five to six years in order to allow time for any civil litigation).

A RIDDOR report must be received by the UK HSE within ten days of the incident, save for over-seven-day incapacitation of a worker (which must be received within fifteen days). There is no requirement under RIDDOR to report incidents of disease or deaths of members of the public, patients, care home residents or service users from COVID-19. The reporting requirements relating to cases of, or deaths from, COVID-19 under RIDDOR apply only to occupational exposure, that is, directly as a result of a person's work (which will only be relevant in most cases in a healthcare environment).

In Northern Ireland, the RIDDOR (Northern Ireland) 1997 is the applicable legislation.

13.7. Workplace Violence

The HSE defines work-related violence as any 'incident in which a person is abused, threatened or assaulted in circumstances relating to their work'. Work-related violence may in some cases by RIDDOR reportable.

13.8. Fines and Penalties

Health and safety inspectors have a wider range of enforcement powers and options including:

- providing information and advice face-to-face or in writing;
- serving notices on duty holders;
- withdrawing approvals;
- varying licenses, conditions or exemptions;
- issuing simple cautions;
- prosecution.

The HSE can serve the following formal notices on employers without going to court:

- *Notices of contravention:* A notification of contravention is a document or letter that tells an employer about health and safety laws the HSE thinks that the employer has broken. A notice of contravention tells an employer what they believe needs to be done to remedy the potential breach of law. An inspector will serve a notice of contravention where they consider an employer to be in 'material breach' of the law. This means the inspector thinks an employer has broken the law seriously enough for them to write to an employer about it. Where a notice of contravention is served, there is often a Fee for Intervention involved too (meaning the employer may need to pay for the HSE's time in investigating the breach).

- *Improvement notices:* These require the employer to remedy a fault or institute a programme of work within twenty-one days if, in the opinion of the inspector, the employer is (a) contravening one or more of the relevant statutory provisions, or (b) has contravened one or more of those provisions in circumstances that make it likely that the contravention will continue or be repeated.
- *Prohibition notices (immediate or deferred):* These require an activity (either carried on or likely to be carried on) which, in the inspector's opinion, involves a risk of serious personal injury. There is no requirement for a specific breach of the HSWA 1974 or related regulations.

Breaches of the HSWA 1974 not only carry financial penalties but also may result in prison sentences and potentially an unlimited fine.

13.9. Checklist of Dos and Don'ts

- Ensure that there is a policy on health and safety at work and that risk assessments have been carried out to ensure that hazards are identified, and risk controls can be implemented. These should be reviewed on an appropriate basis.
- Provide the rights types of welfare, health and safety facilities and equipment.
- Decide who in the organization is to be responsible for health and safety (and ensure they have the right competencies to fulfil this role).
- Decide on the method of recording injuries and accidents at work and ensure that RIDDOR reportable injuries are reported within specified time limits to the HSE.
- Ensure that employees understand the hazards to their health and safety within the workplace, including providing them with appropriate training, information and consulting with them about risks they feel are relevant to their employment.
- Make suitable arrangements for first aid, accidents and ill health.
- Ensure that adequate insurance is in place.
- Pay attention to the latest HSE and industry guidance.

14. IMMIGRATION, SECONDMENT AND FOREIGN ASSIGNMENT

14.1. Overview of Laws Controlling Immigration

On 31 January 2020, the UK left the European Union (EU) and following the end of the agreed 'Transition Period' on 31 December 2020, EU free movement rules now longer apply in the UK. The European Economic Area (EEA) and Swiss nationals who arrive in the UK after 31 December 2020 now require a work visa and permission to work in the UK. EEA and Swiss nationals who were already resident in the UK by 11 pm on 31 December 2020 are required to apply for UK immigration status under the EU Settlement Scheme by the deadline of 30 June 2021 to maintain their residence rights in the UK.

All non-British or Irish nationals, including EEA and Swiss nationals who move to the UK after 1 January 2021 will generally need to apply for work permission under the UK's new points-based immigration regime. Under the new regime, work visas generally fall under the following key categories:

- Employer sponsored visa routes: includes Skilled Worker visas for new hires coming to fill a genuine vacancy and Intra Company Transfer visas for secondments and transfers from the employer's linked overseas office. These routes require sponsorship by an employer who must hold an immigration sponsorship licence.
- Entrepreneurs routes: covers Innovator, Start-up and Global Talent visas which require endorsement by a designated endorsing body.
- Temporary workers and youth mobility routes: covers temporary work such as internships and work experience programmes as well as youth mobility scheme visas.
- Investor route: which requires a minimum of GBP 2 million investment in the UK.

14.2. Recruiting, Screening and Hiring Process

Individuals subject to UK immigration control are required to hold a visa with appropriate work permission to undertake the job in question. Employers in the UK have a duty to prevent illegal working and should ensure they have suitable processes in place to check the right to work of all prospective employees before the start of the employment. Offers of employment made should be conditional upon the prospective employee providing suitable evidence of right to work in the UK at or before the start of employment.

To avoid exposure to possible discrimination claims, employers should ensure the same right to work checks are undertaken on all applicants at the same stage of the recruitment process. When checking right to work documents, an employer must take reasonable steps to verify the authenticity of the documents, including by checking that any photograph or date of birth accords with the apparent appearance and age of the individual. The employer should also check the expiry dates of any visas held and where relevant, ensure follow up right to work checks are undertaken in respect of time limited visas. Evidence of the right to work check undertaken including a record of the documents checked should be retained on file.

British citizens are not subject to immigration control in the UK; however, citizens of British Dependent Territories and British Overseas citizens do require immigration permission to work in the UK. Nationals of EEA countries and Switzerland arriving in the UK from January 2021 onwards are required to obtain permission to work under the new points-based system.

Business visitors can come to the UK for up to six months in order to undertake certain prescribed business activities (e.g., attending meetings, signing contracts, taking instructions from a client or customer in respect of a project or contract to be undertaken from outside the UK). In practice, most business visits will be much shorter (i.e., days or weeks) and visitors are not permitted to undertake anything which amounts to productive work while in the UK, whether this is paid or unpaid. Business visitors must be prepared to satisfy UK immigration authorities as to the purpose and intended duration of their visit as well as the proposed business activities to be undertaken.

14.3. Obligation of Employer to Enforce Immigration Laws

The law on preventing illegal working is set out in sections 15–25 of the Immigration, Asylum and Nationality Act 2006 (the 2006 Act), section 24B of the Immigration Act 1971, and Schedule 6 of the Immigration Act 2016. An employer commits a civil offence and is liable to pay a civil penalty up to GBP 20,000 per illegal worker if it employs a person aged 16 or over who is subject to immigration control and who has no permission to work in the UK, or who works for the employer in breach of their conditions of stay in the UK.

Where appropriate right to work checks have been undertaken before the start of employment, the employer will have a 'statutory excuse' (i.e., a defence) against a civil penalty for illegal working. The level of the civil penalty will be assessed on a sliding scale, taking into account a number of factors including the nature and extent of the right to work checks undertaken by the employer, and the employer's cooperation as well as any previous immigration offences within the preceding three years.

An employer will commit a criminal offence if it knowingly or has reasonable cause to believe that it is employing someone who does not have permission to work in the UK. Employers, convicted of employing an illegal migrant worker will also be subject to criminal penalties, including up to five years of imprisonment and/or an unlimited fine. There is no statutory defence to the criminal penalty. Immigration officers have powers of arrest, entry and search.

Where the employer is registered as a licenced sponsor and fails to comply with the UK immigration rules, UKVI could take action which could lead to its sponsor licence being downgraded or revoked. If the licence is revoked, the employer will no longer be able to sponsor overseas employees and existing sponsored employees would have their visas curtailed (cancelled).

14.4. Fines and Penalties

There is a civil penalty for employing workers illegally, of up to GBP 20,000 per illegal worker (*see* above). An employer who knowingly employs an illegal worker commits a criminal offence and the potential fines are unlimited.

14.5. Secondment/Foreign Assignment

Employers are able to temporarily second existing employees from linked overseas entities to take up a skilled role in the UK under the intra-company category of the points-based system. Applicants must score the minimum level of points under the specified characteristics to qualify and they must be paid at or above the specified rate for the job type.

14.6. Checklist of Dos and Don'ts

- Employers should ensure right to work checks are undertaken in respect of prospective employees at the same point in the recruitment process to ensure that they have the correct right to work in the UK for the job in question.
- Employers should carry out follow up right to work checks where relevant to verify employees on time limited UK visas continue to have the right to work in the UK.

15. RESTRICTIVE COVENANTS AND PROTECTION OF TRADE SECRETS AND CONFIDENTIAL INFORMATION

15.1. Overview

Only highly confidential information amounting to a trade secret will be protected by common law. Employers who wish to protect wider categories of confidential information will need to ensure they include a confidentiality provision in the employment contract (or in a separate confidentiality or non-disclosure agreement).

Employees are not restricted from competing with their employer, or poaching clients or staff, after they leave employment, unless there are express restrictive covenants in the employment contract (or any settlement agreement entered into in connection with the termination of their employment).

15.2. The Law of Trade Secrets

The category into which the relevant piece of information falls will govern the extent to which its owner can protect that information as well as the remedies available to it in the event of its disclosure.

Information which amounts to a trade secret can be protected both during and after the termination of employment, even if there is not an express covenant in an employment contract. Examples of trade secrets include highly secret product information and customer databases. Employers may seek an injunction and/or damages if an employee uses or discloses trade secrets during or after employment.

In contrast, confidential information which is not a trade secret can only be protected with an express contractual provision. Examples of confidential information include details of company finances and prospective business transactions.

Those attempting to protect confidential information should be as familiar as possible with the information itself, its purpose and its constituent parts. It is common for legal advisors simply to define 'confidential information' using pre-prepared lists of information that is likely to be confidential when drafting an employment contract or confidentiality agreement.

Simply defining information as 'confidential' will not, however, be enough to make it so. The courts will examine the information, its provenance and purpose, and the damage it could do (or has done) to its owner if it were disclosed without authorization. They will then use this factual matrix to determine the proper status of the information and the type and extent of protection to be afforded to it.

15.3. Restrictive Covenants and Non-compete Agreements

15.3.1. Overview

A contractual term restricting an employee's activities after termination is void for being in restraint of trade and contrary to the public policy unless the employer can show that it is no wider than necessary to protect a legitimate interest. The legitimate interests which are capable of protection are:

- Confidential information.
- Trade connections (with customers, clients or suppliers).
- Stability of the workforce.

There can be no guarantee that any restrictive covenant will be enforceable, and there are no general guidelines which can be specified as to what would be considered reasonable, for example, in terms of time or geography. Each clause must be considered in each case by reference to the business needs of the employer imposing the restriction.

There is no need to assign specific payments to restrictive covenants in an employment contract in order to make them enforceable. Where the covenants are contained in a contract of employment signed at the start of the employment relationship the employee's salary and benefits will act as sufficient consideration. If restrictive covenants are introduced later, for example, when an employee is promoted, new consideration should be provided. If there is any doubt over whether consideration has been provided, the usual solution is to execute the relevant document (e.g., a variation of the existing employment contract which contains new restrictive covenants) as a deed.

Note that consideration is not required under Scots law for the covenant to be enforceable.

There is no requirement under UK law to pay an employee during the period of the restrictive covenant, and it would be unusual for a covenant to provide for this.

15.3.2. Duration and Geography

When deciding the appropriate period for which an employee will be restricted for, it is necessary to consider how long it will be before competitive activities by the individual represent less than a material threat to the legitimate interest. For example, how long will it be before the manufacturing process changes so much that the individual's knowledge of it is out of date? A longer lasting restriction represents a greater restraint of trade and therefore will be less likely to be enforceable. As a broad rule of thumb, the longest period a court would usually be prepared to enforce a covenant for is twelve months, but in many cases a shorter period would be more appropriate. If the contract contains a garden leave clause this will also be a relevant consideration when deciding enforceability (*see* below).

The geographical extent of the limitation must also be considered. A restriction that covers a wider geographical area necessarily represents a greater restraint of trade and therefore will be less likely to be enforceable. Relevant factors in determining whether the geographical scope is reasonable will include the area of activities of the employer and the size and nature of the population of the area.

15.3.3. Types of Covenants

Non-solicitation/Dealing with Clients/Customers

Client/customer covenants should be restricted to clients/customers with whom the employee had contact during a specified period before termination, and should also be restricted to dealings with clients/customers in relation to similar products or services supplied by the employer. The appropriate period of the covenant is usually the length of time that it would reasonably take for the replacement employee to establish a relationship with the clients/customers. Typically these covenants last for a period of six to twelve months.

Non-solicitation/Dealing with Employees

As with the client/customer covenants, employee covenants should also be restricted to cover only colleagues with whom the employee had contact during a specified period before termination. The appropriate period of the covenant is usually the length of time it would reasonably take for the employee's replacement to establish a relationship with the team, and typically would be a period of six to twelve months.

Non-compete Covenants

A non-compete covenant will often be harder to enforce than a client/customer or employee restriction since it represents a greater restriction on the employee. However, courts are prepared to enforce non-compete covenants where they are reasonably necessary to protect a legitimate interest, which will typically be confidential information, but the covenant may also be used to protect relationships with clients/customers.

Non-compete covenants should ideally last for a shorter period than other covenants, to give them more chance of being enforceable. For example, it is not uncommon to see a period of six months for a non-compete covenant, with client/customer and employee covenants lasting for twelve months (although in some cases shorter periods are more appropriate such as three months and six months).

15.3.4. Garden Leave

Another way in which employers can protect their business from competition from a departing employee is with a garden leave clause. This clause allows the employer to require the employee to stay away from work, and not contact clients or colleagues, during the notice period. The period of garden leave should ideally be set off against the period that any restrictive covenants run for, so, for example, if an employee had a six-month notice period and a twelve-month non-solicitation of clients covenant, this covenant should be reduced to six months. Care should be taken when drafting covenants to ensure that any period of garden leave is taken into account in this way.

15.4. Checklist of Dos and Don'ts

Dos

- Ensure that the drafting of restrictive covenants is aimed at protecting legitimate business interests and not simply at preventing competition.
- Include appropriate limits in restrictive covenants in terms of time and geographical scope as well as the clients/customers and or employees that the employee is restricted from soliciting or dealing with.
- Consider which posts bring employees into contact with customers and clients and/or expose them to confidential information (particularly the type that could damage the business if disclosed), and draft appropriate covenants into those employees' contracts.
- Include a garden leave clause in the contract and generally provide that any restricted period is reduced by time spent on garden leave.

Don'ts

- Avoid adopting a blanket system of including standard form restrictive covenants in all employee contracts – tailor them to the role.

16. PROTECTION OF WHISTLEBLOWING CLAIMS

16.1. Overview

Whistleblower protection is provided by the Public Interest Disclosure Act 1998, which amended the ERA 1996. The applicable legislation in Northern Ireland is the Public Interest Disclosure (Northern Ireland) Order 1998, the Employment Rights (Northern Ireland) Order 1996 (as amended), and the Employment Act (Northern Ireland) 2016, (Commencement Number One) Order (Northern Ireland) 2017.

Whistleblowing laws provide protection to employees and workers from being dismissed or subjected to a detriment because they have made a 'protected disclosure' (*see* below).

Dismissal of an employee will be deemed automatically unfair if the reason, or principal reason, is that they have made a protected disclosure. Unlike in an ordinary unfair dismissal claim, if a whistleblowing unfair dismissal claim succeeds there is no limit on the compensation that can be awarded (though it is still based on the employee's losses). Also, unlike ordinary unfair dismissal for which an employee needs to have two years' service, there is no minimum service requirement to bring a whistleblowing unfair dismissal claim.

It is unlawful for an employer to subject a worker to a detriment on the ground that they have made a protected disclosure. There is no limit on the amount of compensation that can be awarded to the detriment. Compensation is also available for injury to feelings in a detriment claim (but not in a dismissal claim).

A worker qualifies for whistleblower protection if they have made a 'protected disclosure' in accordance with the legislation. In order to be protected the disclosure must be a disclosure of information which in the reasonable belief of the worker is made in the public interest and concerns:

- a criminal offence;
- a breach of any legal obligation;
- a miscarriage of justice;
- danger to health and safety;
- damage to the environment, or
- a deliberate cover-up of any of the above.

In addition, the disclosure must be made either to the employer or to a regulator (such as the Financial Conduct Authority).

The disclosure must be a disclosure of information (this can be done in writing or verbally) but merely gathering evidence, raising an allegation or threatening to make a disclosure is not sufficient.

Many employers have introduced whistleblowing or 'speak up' policies encouraging disclosure of matters internally, and in the financial services sector it is a regulatory requirement to have whistleblowing policies and procedures. It is good practice for employers to offer a number of different channels to employees for raising concerns, including anonymous whistleblowing hotlines operated by external providers.

16.2. Checklist of Dos and Don'ts

- Have a clear and easily understandable whistleblowing/speak up policy covering how employees should raise issues should they wish to 'blow the whistle' and complain about working practices or other matters.
- Make sure all employees are aware of the policy and that it is easily accessible to them.
- Consider having multiple ways for employees to raise concerns, including a method which is anonymous (e.g., an anonymous whistleblowing hotline).
- Promote a working culture whereby employees feel that they can raise concerns without fear of adverse reactions or consequences.
- Provide training to the workforce on the whistleblowing procedure and make sure that managers are trained on how to recognize and deal with a whistleblowing complaint.
- Do not punish an employee or subject them to any detriment as a result of blowing the whistle and ensure that employees know that doing so is not acceptable and will be a disciplinary matter.

17. PROHIBITION OF DISCRIMINATION IN THE WORKPLACE

17.1. Overview of Discrimination Laws

Summary

Discrimination law prohibits discrimination on a number of different grounds, in all facets of employment including recruitment, contractual terms, working conditions, promotions, transfers, dismissals and training.

The law in GB is contained in the EqA 2010. The principal legislation relating to employment equality in Northern Ireland is the Fair Employment and Treatment (Northern Ireland) Order 1998. In addition, Northern Ireland has separate statutes dealing with the areas of race, sex, sexual orientation, disability and age discrimination. (The Fair Employment and Treatment

(Northern Ireland) Order 1998 places a number of significant duties on employers that are not found in other anti-discrimination legislation either in Northern Ireland or in GB. For further information refer to section 3 above.)

Discrimination laws protect employees (in a broad sense), former employees and applicants for employment. The term 'employment' is defined for the purposes of discrimination law as working under a contract of service or apprenticeship, or a contract personally to perform any work. As such, as well as including employees and workers, it also covers those who are genuinely self-employed, provided the contract obliges them to perform the work personally (in other words, if they are not permitted to subcontract any part of the work or employ their own staff to do it). The wide definition of employment can therefore encompass a broad range of non-employed individuals, such as agency workers, office-holders and partners.

While the law primarily governs the conduct of employers, others (including individual employees, managers and agents of the employer) may also be held personally liable where they have played a part in the discrimination. An employer may have a defence in respect of the discriminatory actions of an employee if it can demonstrate that it took all reasonable steps to prevent the employee from engaging in the discriminatory act or anything of that description.

The EqA also prohibits discrimination in goods, facilities and services, which are outside the scope of this note.

Discrimination in Employment

In terms of employment-related discrimination, an employer must not discriminate against an employee in any of the following ways:

- On recruitment, both in terms of offering employment and as regards the contractual terms of employment offered.
- In access to opportunities for promotion, transfer or training (internal promotion poses a risk of unlawful discrimination as often it involves subjective managerial assessment).
- In access to any other benefits, facilities or services including pay, holiday, pension, and other fringe benefits such as opportunities to work overtime. It can also relate to a failure to deal with an employee's grievance adequately or dealing with an employee's grievance but with an unreasonable amount of delay.
- By dismissing an employee. This includes termination of a contract by the employer (with or without notice) and non-renewal or expiry of a fixed-term contract. Criteria used for dismissal, including in selection for redundancies, must not be directly or indirectly discriminatory.
- By subjecting the employee to any other detriment.

Grounds for Discrimination

The protection against discrimination relates to specified 'protected characteristics', namely:

- Age
- Disability
- Gender reassignment
- Marriage and civil partnership
- Pregnancy and maternity
- Race
- Religion or belief
- Sex
- Sexual orientation.

It is interesting to note that the protected characteristic does not need to relate to the person complaining of discrimination. Discrimination by association and perception can also be covered. However, an employee who has experienced detrimental treatment on other grounds not falling within the protected characteristics (such as socio-economic status or regional, as opposed to national, origin) would not be protected by the laws on discrimination.

Discrimination may be permitted in certain limited circumstances. For example:

- an employer might be able to rely on a genuine occupational requirement for an employee to possess a particular protected characteristic (such as an actor of a certain race being cast to play a character of that same race); and
- 'positive discrimination' is permitted where two candidates for recruitment or promotion are equally qualified and the employer selects one of them in order to help redress any under-representation in the workforce (*see* section 24 below).

Direct Discrimination

Direct discrimination occurs where a person treats another person less favourably because of one of the protected characteristics listed above (e.g., race or sex), compared with someone else without that characteristic (a comparator).

The comparator must be someone whose 'relevant circumstances are the same or not materially different'. There may be an actual comparator or the employee can bring a claim based on a 'hypothetical comparator'.

The only exception to the rule requiring a comparator for direct discrimination is with pregnancy and maternity discrimination, where there is no need for a comparator because the employee need only show she was treated 'unfavourably' due to her pregnancy or maternity leave.

With the exception of age discrimination, direct discrimination cannot be generally be justified. In the case of disability discrimination, someone who is not disabled cannot complain of discrimination in respect of more favourable treatment given to disabled persons. Similarly, in the context of sex discrimination, it is permissible to afford a woman special treatment in connection with pregnancy or childbirth.

Indirect Discrimination

Indirect discrimination occurs where:

- an employer applies a provision criterion or practice (PCP) to the whole workforce, or to part of the workforce which disproportionately adversely affects individuals with a particular protected characteristic; and
- the PCP cannot be objectively justified.

A common example of possible indirect discrimination is an employer requiring all employees to work full time. This requirement has a disproportionate impact on women, since women are statistically more likely to have primary caring responsibilities. An employer would need to objectively justify such a policy.

In order to justify a PCP, the employer has to show that it is a proportionate means of achieving a legitimate aim. For example, the employer may seek to justify a policy of full-time working in order to deliver a consistent service to clients, but in order to do so it would have to demonstrate that there this could not be achieved any other way, for example, with a well-organized job share.

Victimization

The prohibition on victimization is intended to ensure that victims and witnesses are not deterred from speaking out against discrimination or harassment for fear of reprisals.

Victimization occurs where an employer subjects an individual a detriment in connection with their doing a 'protected act', namely:

- bringing discrimination or equal pay proceedings;
- giving evidence or information in connection with discrimination or equal pay proceedings brought by someone else;
- alleging discrimination or breach of equal pay legislation;
- doing anything else by reference to the discrimination or equal pay legislation.

Making an allegation or giving information that later turns out to be false can still constitute a protected act, provided it was done in good faith. In contrast, making a discrimination allegation with no merit brought solely to harass the employer is not a protected act, as it is not brought in good faith.

Victimization is usually committed by an employer who has been the subject of a discrimination complaint by a current or former employee, but this need not always be the case. For example, a prospective new employer can be liable for victimization if it refuses to employ someone who has given evidence against a previous employer in a discrimination case.

Harassment

Harassment is unwanted conduct which is related to protected characteristic; and has the purpose or effect of violating the victim's dignity or creating an intimidating, hostile, degrading, humiliating or offensive environment for the victim.

In deciding what effect the conduct had on the victim the Employment Tribunal will take into account the victim's subjective perception of the conduct and also objectively whether in all the circumstances it was reasonable for the conduct to have that effect.

Protection from harassment extends to the following protected characteristics: age; disability; gender reassignment; race; religion or belief; sex and sexual orientation. Pregnancy and maternity, and marriage and civil partnership are not covered. However, in practice it is possible that actions taken in connection with those protected characteristics might be capable of protection under the wider category of 'sex'.

Bringing a Discrimination Claim

A discrimination claim must usually be submitted to an employment tribunal before the end of 'the period of three months beginning when the act complained of was done' (the normal time limit). Acts occurring more than three months before the claim is brought may still form the basis of the claim if they are part of a 'continuing act'. Regardless of whether there is a continuing act, time can be extended by the tribunal where it is just and equitable to do so.

The task of proving a discrimination case lies initially on the claimant. They must prove facts from which the tribunal could conclude, in the absence of an adequate explanation, that the respondent has committed an act of unlawful discrimination or harassment (the 'prima facie' case). The claim will succeed unless the employer can prove that it did not discriminate against the claimant.

In a successful discrimination claim, an Employment Tribunal will award compensation for the employee's financial losses (including loss of earnings, pension, and benefits in kind and any out-of-pocket expenses). There is no limit on the amount which may be awarded, although since the amount is loss based it will depend on how much the employee earned and how long it will take them to find new employment with similar earnings.

The Employment Tribunal will also award an amount for injury to feelings, which may be between GBP 900 and GBP 45,600, depending on the severity of the case.

If the employee remains in employment, the Tribunal may also make recommendations as to what steps the employer should take to avoid future discrimination.

Compensation can be awarded against the employer and against any individual respondents, such as other employees.

17.2. Age Discrimination

Age discrimination applies to vocational training and all facets of employment. The protections outlined above against direct and indirect discrimination, victimization and harassment all apply to the protected characteristic of age. However, unlike other protected characteristics, direct age discrimination can be justified where the age-based criterion is a proportionate means of achieving a legitimate aim.

Discrimination on the grounds of age may be permitted in certain limited circumstances, such as to award benefits based on length of service. Where a length of service requirement exceeds five years, the employer needs to have a reasonable belief that the requirement 'fulfils a business need'.

Note that there is no longer an exception to permit termination of an employee's employment on reaching retirement age. Accordingly, attempts to enforce a retirement age would constitute direct age discrimination. While this could technically be objectively justified, in practice most employers have not sought to rely on this, in part because it may be difficult to demonstrate for the purposes of objective justification that the chosen retirement age is a proportionate one.

The applicable legislation in Northern Ireland is the Employment Equality (Age) Regulations (Northern Ireland) 2006.

17.3. Race Discrimination

It is unlawful to discriminate against someone on racial grounds such as colour, race, nationality or ethnic or national origins. The protections outlined above against direct and indirect discrimination, victimization and harassment all apply to the protected characteristic of race.

It is clear from case law that 'ethnic origin' is wider than 'racial origin'. Discrimination against a member of an ethnic group can be taken as encompassing religious and cultural differences as well as strictly racial differences.

The applicable legislation in Northern Ireland is the Race Relations (Northern Ireland) Order 1997 (which in addition to race also deals with travellers in Northern Ireland).

17.4. Sex Discrimination/Sexual Harassment

The protections outlined above against direct and indirect discrimination, victimization and harassment all apply to the protected characteristic of sex.

In the context of harassment, the EqA also sets out particular protections in relation to sexual harassment. Sexual harassment is defined as unwanted conduct of a sexual nature, which has the purpose or effect of violating the victim's dignity or creating an intimidating, hostile, degrading, humiliating or offensive environment for the victim.

In addition to sex discrimination, the EqA also contains separate provisions relating to equal pay for equal work. Equal pay claims are complex in nature, partly because it can be difficult to establish whether two employees are carrying out equal work, and also because there are often many different factors which determine how much an individual is paid.

The applicable legislation is the Sex Discrimination (Northern Ireland) Order 1976 (as amended).

17.5. Handicap and Disability Discrimination

The EqA in GB, and Disability Discrimination Act 1995 in Northern Ireland, prohibits discrimination against those with disabilities and creates certain obligations on employers in relation to an employee with a disability. A person has a disability if they have a physical or mental impairment which has a substantial and long-term effect on their ability to carry out normal day-to-day activities. For these purposes, 'long term' is defined as an impairment that has lasted, or is likely to last for at least twelve months.

While there are some similarities in approach to other strands of discrimination law, there are two significant differences:

(1) Only persons with a condition falling within the definition of 'disability' set out in EqA qualify for its protection.

(2) Uniquely in domestic discrimination law, it imposes obligations on employers to treat disabled persons more favourably in certain circumstances.

In addition to protection from direct discrimination, indirect discrimination, harassment and victimization (as outlined above), the EqA also provides for the following disability-specific protections:

- Discrimination arising from disability.
- Failure to comply with a duty to make reasonable adjustments.

Discrimination Arising from Disability

Discrimination arising from disability occurs where a person is treated unfavourably for a reason related to their disability, and the treatment is not objectively justified. For example, if an employer seeks to issue a disciplinary warning or to dismiss for high levels of absence, this may constitute discrimination arising from disability if the absences are a consequence of the disability and the employer cannot show that the action taken is justified as a proportionate means of achieving a legitimate aim.

An employer faced with a claim of discrimination arising from disability has a defence if they did not know, and could not reasonably have been expected to know, that the employee had the disability.

Failure to Comply with a Duty to Make a Reasonable Adjustment

The law imposes a duty on employers to make reasonable adjustments to premises or working practices to accommodate a disabled employee or job applicant. The duty is to take such steps as it is reasonable, in all the circumstances of the case, taking into account the employer's size and resources, and the extent to which the adjustments would benefit the employee.

A claim can be brought for a breach of this duty. In addition, an employer will not be able to justify disability-related discrimination (*see* above) where there were reasonable adjustments which could have been made, unless the employer shows that, even with those adjustments, the discrimination would still have been justified.

17.6. National Origin Discrimination

The law prohibits discrimination on the grounds of nationality, which is defined to include citizenship (and more widely falls within the protected characteristic of 'race' – *see* above). It is not limited to the legal nationality acquired at birth but can include a change in nationality, e.g., due to marriage.

The applicable legislation in Northern Ireland is the Race Relations (Northern Ireland) Order 1997 (which in addition to race also deals with travellers in Northern Ireland).

17.7. Religious Discrimination

The protections outlined above against direct and indirect discrimination, victimization and harassment all apply to the protected characteristic of religion and belief. 'Religion or belief' means any religion and any religious or philosophical belief.

In recent times, there has been a significant amount of press given to discrimination cases involving religion and belief. These have largely centred on two distinct themes:

(1) the potential for conflict between the laws prohibiting discrimination on the grounds of religion or belief and sexual orientation (e.g., where a religious belief does not accommodate homosexuality). In these cases, the courts have tended to seek to strike a balance between affording protection to those with a particular religion or belief, while drawing a line where the practice or manifestation of that religion or belief encroaches on the rights of others;

(2) the question of what can constitute a 'belief'. Most recently, it was determined that ethical veganism is capable of constituting a belief. However, this is not a blanket determination such that all vegans would be protected. Rather, the determination would still need to be made on a case by case basis by reference to the individual's own beliefs and the way in which those beliefs are manifested in daily life (e.g., the belief would need to be sufficiently weighty and cogent – akin to a religious belief).

Beyond the standard exceptions for permitted areas of discrimination, there are some additional exceptions that apply in the context of religion and belief. For example, religious organizations may be able to defend a requirement for an employee to be of a particular sexual orientation in some circumstances. Also, organizations with a religious ethos may be able to stipulate that certain roles must be held by individuals who follow their religion (e.g., a Catholic counselling service may be able to require that its counsellors are Catholic).

The applicable legislation in Northern Ireland is the Fair Employment and Treatment (Northern Ireland) Order 1989. This specific piece of legislation in Northern Ireland which deals with discrimination on the grounds of religious belief and/or political opinion has no direct equivalent in GB. The remit of the legislation is much wider, and it has the power to impose obligations and sanctions on employers who fail to meet its standards.

17.8. Military Status Discrimination

In the UK there is no specific protection against discrimination on the grounds of military or veteran status.

17.9. Pregnancy and Maternity Discrimination

The protections described above for direct and indirect discrimination and harassment do not apply in the same way to pregnancy and maternity. Instead, there is a dedicated provision pursuant to which an employer discriminates against a woman if, in the protected period in relation to a pregnancy of hers, her employer treats her unfavourably because of her pregnancy, a pregnancy-related illness or maternity leave.

Unlike direct discrimination claims for other protected characteristics, a pregnant employee does not need to demonstrate less favourable treatment by reference to a comparator. Rather, she merely needs to demonstrate 'unfavourable' treatment.

Dismissal for a reason related to pregnancy is automatically unfair, and employees will also be protected from victimization in connection with bringing or supporting a complaint of pregnancy and maternity discrimination (as outlined above).

The applicable legislation in Northern Ireland is the Sex Discrimination (Northern Ireland) Order 1976 (as amended).

17.10. Marital Status Discrimination

The law prohibits direct and indirect discrimination against people of either sex on the grounds of their marital or civil partner status. For example, any benefits such as private medical insurance, provided by employers to employees' spouses must also be extended to employee's civil partners.

There is no parallel protection for unmarried people. There is also no protection against harassment, although depending on the facts it is possible that a person who is married or in a civil partnership might be able to make out a harassment claim under the category of sex or sexual orientation.

The applicable legislation in Northern Ireland is the Sex Discrimination (Northern Ireland) Order 1976 (as amended).

17.11. Sexual Orientation Discrimination

The protections outlined above against direct and indirect discrimination, victimization and harassment all apply to the protected characteristic of sexual orientation.

'Sexual orientation' is defined as a sexual orientation towards persons of the same sex; persons of the opposite sex; or persons of either sex.

There is separate protection, under the separate protected characteristic of 'gender reassignment', for employees who are proposing to undergo, are in the process of undergoing, or have undergone, gender reassignment. The law requires a commitment to transitioning and accordingly transvestites are not protected (unless, for example, they are discriminated against on the basis of perceived gender reassignment). However, the law has not yet caught up to the greater societal understanding around intersex and non-binary individuals, who do not have an express protection from discrimination under the EqA, unless they are able to establish a claim in relation to sexual orientation or gender reassignment (including perceived gender reassignment).

The applicable legislation in Northern Ireland is the Employment Equality (Sexual Orientation) Regulations (Northern Ireland) 2003.

17.12. Retaliation

'Retaliation' is a term that is equivalent to victimization under UK discrimination laws. This is dealt with above.

17.13. Constructive Discharge

Referred to as a constructive dismissal under UK law, this occurs where the employer does not dismiss the employee, but breaches the employment contract entitling the employee to resign, and the employee is therefore treated as though they were dismissed and can bring claims accordingly. Acts of discrimination and harassment almost invariably entitle an employee to resign and claim to have been constructively dismissed.

The applicable legislation in Northern Ireland is the Employment Rights (Northern Ireland) Order 1996. The qualifying period for unfair dismissal and constructive unfair dismissal rights in Northern Ireland is one year (in contrast to the two-year qualifying period in GB).

17.14. Checklist of Dos and Don'ts

- Adopt equal opportunities and anti-harassment policies dealing with all aspects of discrimination in the workplace.
- Ensure that managers and staff are trained on equal opportunity issues in the workplace and their obligations, including on the effects of unconscious bias.
- Implement appropriate 'speak up' or whistleblowing avenues to ensure that employees feel able to raise concerns, and to help demonstrate a culture which does not lend itself to victimizing those who complain.

18. SMOKING IN THE WORKPLACE

18.1. Overview

A ban on smoking in enclosed and substantially enclosed workplaces and other public places was introduced in England on 1 July 2007 under the Health Act 2006. Similar bans were introduced in Northern Ireland and Wales in April 2007 and in Scotland in March 2006.

Almost all workplaces are covered by the smoking ban and must be kept smoke-free at all times. Workplaces are covered if they are enclosed or substantially enclosed – i.e., premises with a ceiling or roof where the aggregate area of openings (excluding windows and doors) is less than half the total wall area. Work vehicles are also covered by the ban (including all vehicles used in the course of work by more than one person, even if those persons use the vehicle at different times).

Under the smoking ban, employers have a duty to prevent smoking in the workplace and must also display prescribed no-smoking signs in their premises and in work vehicles. It is a criminal offence for any individual to smoke in the workplace and it is also an offence for the employer (or any person in charge of the premises) to fail to prevent smoking in the workplace or to fail to ensure appropriate no-smoking signs are displayed. The maximum penalty for an employer who fails to prevent smoking in the workplace is GBP 2,500, and the maximum penalty for failing to display no-smoking signs is GBP 1,000. An employer charged with the offence of failing to prevent smoking in the workplace will have a defence if it can show: (a) it took reasonable steps to prevent smoking; (b) that it did not know, and could not reasonably be expected to know, that there were people smoking; or (c) there were other grounds why it was not reasonable to comply with the duty.

18.2. Checklist of Dos and Don'ts

- Employers should implement a 'no-smoking' policy and ensure all staff and visitors to the workplace are aware of it.
- Employers should ensure appropriate 'no-smoking' signs are displayed in the workplace and in work vehicles.
- Disciplinary policies should refer to smoking as gross misconduct which is potentially punishable by summary dismissal.

19. USE OF DRUGS AND ALCOHOL IN THE WORKPLACE

19.1. Overview of Laws and Regulations

There are no specific laws or regulations dealing with drugs and alcohol in the workplace. However, there are various laws and regulations which are relevant, and the interaction of these laws can create complex issues for employers. The following laws will be particularly relevant:

- the HSWA 1974 and its related regulations, which impose a duty on employers to ensure, so far as is reasonably practicable, the health, safety and welfare of employees at work;
- the ERA 1996 which sets out the unfair dismissal regime and will impact on the fairness of any dismissal related to drugs and alcohol;
- the EqA 2010 which prohibits discrimination on various grounds, including disability;
- the Data Protection Act 2018 (DPA) which governs the processing of employees' personal data and will be relevant to any requirement for employees to undergo drugs and alcohol testing; and
- the Misuse of Drugs Act 1971, under which employers can themselves potentially commit an offence if they know that illegal drugs are being used or distributed on their premises and take no action.

In Northern Ireland, the key legislation is:

- the Health and Safety at Work (Northern Ireland) Order 1978;
- the Management of Health and Safety at Work Regulations (Northern Ireland) 2000; and
- the Employment Rights (Northern Ireland) Order 1996 which sets out the unfair dismissal law applicable in Northern Ireland and will impact the fairness of any dismissal related to drugs and alcohol.

The use or possession of illegal drugs or alcohol by an employee in the workplace will often be clear grounds for disciplinary action, particularly where this would pose a risk to the health and safety of the employee or others. The use of illegal drugs or alcohol outside of work may also give the employer grounds for disciplinary action where there is some impact on the workplace, e.g., it affects the employee's conduct or performance, it presents a safety risk to the employee or others, or it has the potential to bring the employer's business into disrepute.

Despite this, there is a developing body of case law and guidance in the UK that suggests that employers should treat the long-term misuse of illegal drugs and alcohol as a health problem and, where possible, offer support to encourage the employee to seek help and treatment (with disciplinary action being used as a last resort). Often a distinction is drawn between a one-off incident of misuse (which is more likely to be treated as a disciplinary issue) and a longer-term dependency or addiction (which is more likely to be treated as a health issue). The treatment will be relevant in determining whether any dismissal related to drugs or alcohol is fair under the ERA.

The treatment may also be relevant under the EqA. Addictions to alcohol, nicotine or non-prescription drugs are specifically excluded from constituting disabilities and are therefore outside of the scope of the EqA's protection against disability discrimination. However, alcoholism or drug dependence could be a symptom of another underlying health condition (e.g., depression) or could give rise to a health condition (e.g., cardiovascular disease) which may constitute a disability under the EqA.

Employers should have clear policies on the implications for staff of drug and alcohol use and misuse both inside and outside the workplace. Such policies should also explain the circumstances in which employees may be subject to drug and alcohol testing.

Drug and Alcohol Testing

The employer's right to require employees to undergo drugs or alcohol testing is limited. As a minimum, the right should be set out in the employment contract or staff handbook or policy. Even then, employers should only use testing where necessary, e.g., to ensure the health and safety of staff and others. Given the intrusive nature of testing, employers will need to ensure that any testing complies with the DPA and employees' right to privacy under Human Rights legislation.

The UK's Information Commissioner (the data protection regulatory body) has produced an Employment Practices Code which provides guidance on, among other things, drug and alcohol testing by employers. The Code highlights the importance of explaining, in a staff handbook or policy, the reasons for any drug and alcohol testing and the consequences for workers of non-compliance. Workers should also be aware of the circumstances in which any testing may take place, the nature of the testing, how information obtained through testing will be used, and the safeguards that are in place for the personal information of those subject to testing. Testing is more likely to be justified on employees where there is a reasonable suspicion of misuse, rather than where it is done at random. However, where random testing is considered necessary, the Code states that it should be genuinely random as opposed to being targeted at particular workers.

Where a request to undergo testing is reasonable and proportionate in the circumstances, a refusal to comply may amount to misconduct (on the basis that it constitutes a refusal to follow a lawful and reasonable instruction). Conversely, requiring employees to undergo testing without justification is likely to breach the DPA and/or constitute a breach of the implied duty of mutual trust and confidence.

19.2. Checklist of Dos and Don'ts

- Adopt a clear policy on dealing with drugs and alcohol in the workplace, which is clearly communicated to workers.
- Ensure that matters such as drug and alcohol testing and the misuse of drugs and alcohol outside of work are dealt with in the policy.
- Where an employee's alcohol or drug misuse stems from an underlying addiction or other health condition, treat this as a health issue, where possible, and encourage the employee to seek help, with disciplinary action being used as a last resort.
- Only require staff to undergo drug or alcohol testing where there is a clear need and ensure this is done transparently, in the least intrusive way possible.

20. AIDS, HIV, SARS, BLOOD-BORNE PATHOGENS

20.1. Overview

There are no specific employment laws in the UK governing communicable diseases or blood-borne pathogens such as Hepatitis, HIV, AIDS, SARS, MERS or COVID-19. HIV infection is deemed to be a disability under the EqA, meaning that someone who has the infection will be protected by the disability discrimination provisions of the EqA from the point of diagnosis (*see* disability discrimination above).

Employers have a duty to protect the health and safety of their workers under the HSWA 1974. Where a workplace involves activities where there may be contact with blood/body fluids (e.g., in a healthcare setting), a specific risk assessment should be carried out. Suitable prevention and control measures may then need to be put in place. Specific decontamination measures may need to be followed, which will include the appropriate disposal of contaminated waste. Incidents involving these kinds of pathogens and individuals may be RIDDOR reportable. *See* section 13 for further details. The applicable legislation in Northern Ireland is the Health and Safety at Work (Northern Ireland) Order 1978.

In the event of an epidemic or pandemic such as SARS, MERS or COVID-19, employers must be careful to follow guidance from Government, health authorities and other industry stakeholders in order to discharge their health and safety duties fully.

This may include measures such as placing restrictions on business travel to affected areas, mandatory quarantining of exposed staff, additional workplace cleaning and hygiene reminders, and structuring work in a way which allows for social distancing.

20.2. Checklist of Dos and Don'ts

- Consider, with the aid of appropriate medical evidence, whether an employee with a communicable disease or blood-borne pathogen may fall within the definition of disabled under the EqA.
- Implement measures to ensure the health and safety of workers in the event of an instance or outbreak of any communicable disease, taking care to follow Government and health authority guidance.

21. DRESS AND GROOMING REQUIREMENTS

21.1. Overview

Employers can require employees to comply with rules around dress and grooming, but care must be taken to avoid discrimination. Dress codes which disproportionately impact on employees with a protected characteristic will be indirectly discriminatory unless they can be objectively justified (e.g., dress codes in place for health or hygiene reasons). For example, a ban on jewellery could disproportionately affect employees who wear jewellery for religious reasons, and would therefore need to be justified. (*See* section 17 above for more detail on indirect discrimination.)

21.2. Checklist of Dos and Don'ts

- When adopting standards of dress and appearance, ensure that such standards are set out in a policy.
- Assess dress standards for their potential discriminatory effect, and if any of the requirements may have a discriminatory effect, consider whether this is justified or whether the rule should be changed.

22. PRIVACY, TECHNOLOGY AND TRANSFER OF PERSONAL DATA

22.1. Privacy Rights of Employees

Right to Privacy

The Human Rights Act 1998 (HRA) was introduced to give effect in the UK to the rights guaranteed under the European Convention for the Protection of Human Rights and Fundamental Freedoms, including the right to respect for private life.

Public sector employees are able to bring a breach of privacy claim against their employer under the HRA. Employees in the private sector are not able to do this, but the HRA is relevant in relation to other claims they might bring, such as unfair dismissal. This is because Employment Tribunals must take the HRA into account when deciding employment claims.

Monitoring Employees

Issues of privacy tend to arise where an employer is monitoring its employees, such as monitoring email or internet use, or phone calls, or using CCTV or vehicle tracking devices. When monitoring employees, there are various pieces of legislation which employers must comply with, including the GDPR, DPA 2018, and the Telecommunications (Lawful Business Practice) (Interception of Communications) Regulations 2000.

The key principles which employers should comply with in respect of all types of monitoring are:

- Monitoring should only be carried out with a clear purpose and where the employer is satisfied that the monitoring is justified for this purpose.
- Monitoring should be carried out in the least intrusive way possible (e.g., an employer checking for excessive personal use of email should look at email recipients/subjects rather than reading the emails).
- Employees should be made aware that monitoring will take place (except for covert monitoring which is only justified in narrow circumstances).

- Personal information obtained through monitoring should be kept securely and only accessed by employees who need to see it.

There are a number of principles which apply to the processing of personal information by employers, including information collected by monitoring, which are discussed in section 26 below.

22.2. Checklist of Dos and Don'ts

- Consider the purpose of monitoring, whether monitoring is justified and how it can be done in the least intrusive way.
- Ensure that all employees are aware of any monitoring which may take place and the reasons for this, for example, by setting it out in relevant policies such as email and internet policies.
- Put in place processes to ensure that any information collected through monitoring is kept securely and access to it is suitably limited.

23. WORKPLACE INVESTIGATIONS FOR COMPLAINTS OF DISCRIMINATION, HARASSMENT, FRAUD, THEFT AND WHISTLEBLOWING

23.1. Overview

In general, there are no statutory requirements imposing obligations on employers to carry out workplace investigations. However:

- companies subject to financial regulatory obligations will have additional standards to meet in connection with internal complaints and whistleblowing (including requirements as to whistleblowing policies and procedures and reporting requirements), which will inform any investigation process; and
- failure to carry out an investigation, or carrying out an inadequate investigation, may provide grounds for an unfair dismissal claim or lend support to claims for whistleblowing, discrimination or victimization under the EqA.

Additionally, recent trends (such as #metoo) have led to high levels of media scrutiny of the management of complaints raised by employees. Accordingly, there is a greater emphasis on carrying out full and independent investigations into any complaints raised in order to manage legal, regulatory and reputational risk.

The ACAS Code of Practice on Disciplinary and Grievance Procedures sets out guidance for employers on how to investigate and deal with complaints raised under grievance procedures. Failing to comply with the ACAS Code does not, in and of itself, give rise to a claim. However, if an employer unreasonably fails to follow the ACAS Code, an Employment Tribunal is empowered to apply an uplift of up to 25% to an award of compensation in certain cases (such as those relating to unfair dismissal and discrimination).

Employers can obtain advice on carrying out whistleblowing investigations from Protect, the whistleblowing charity.

Northern Ireland

The applicable legislation in Northern Ireland is the Employment Rights (Northern Ireland) Order 1996, the Public Interest Disclosure (Northern Ireland) Order 1998, the Employment Act (Northern Ireland) 2016, (Commencement Number One) Order (Northern Ireland) 2017, and the Fair Employment and Treatment (Northern Ireland) Order 1998. The Northern Ireland employment relations service is the LRA, and it has its own code of practice should formal investigatory, disciplinary, or grievance action be required.

23.2. Checklist of Dos and Don'ts

- Investigation procedures should be set out in policies on harassment, whistleblowing, grievance and disciplinary matters.
- Managers should be trained in conducting investigations.
- Consideration should be given to whether the ACAS Code of Practice applies, and the guidance observed where appropriate.

24. AFFIRMATIVE ACTION/NON-DISCRIMINATION REQUIREMENTS

24.1. Overview

Equality and Human Rights Commission

The EHRC is the statutory body which is responsible for promoting and enforcing equality and diversity in GB. The EHRC's duties include:

- Encouraging good practice in relation to equality and diversity.
- Enforcing discrimination laws and promoting awareness and understanding of them.
- Promoting equality of opportunity.

The EHRC has published the statutory Employment Code of Practice which explains discrimination laws and gives guidance on how to comply with the law. Employment Tribunals are required to take this Code of Practice into account when deciding discrimination claims.

The EHRC can also investigate and take enforcement action in relation to discrimination within an organization, and this is more likely to occur in public sector organizations and/or where significant numbers of employees are affected.

Affirmative Action

In GB, there are some circumstances in which employers may take positive action to improve diversity, but there is no obligation to do so, except for the duty to make reasonable adjustments to accommodate disability (*see* section 17 above).

Employers may take positive action to improve opportunities for individuals with certain protected characteristics (e.g., sex, race) who are under-represented in the workforce or who may be disadvantaged in the workplace, for example, by placing advertisements in certain media outlets, or reserving places on internal training courses for employees from a particular group.

There is only one situation in which positive discrimination is lawful. In a recruitment or promotion scenario, where two individuals are equally qualified for a role, the employer may make the selection based on a protected characteristic, in order to address under-representation either in the workforce generally or at a particular level. For example, if an equally qualified male and female employee applied for promotion to management level, and women were under-represented at management level, the employer could choose the female employee for this reason. In practice, though it is unusual for employers to positively discriminate in this way, because it is rare for two candidates to be genuinely equally qualified, and if they are not then there is a risk of a successful discrimination claim from the losing candidate.

Many employers choose to carry out equal opportunities monitoring, to identify any diversity issues and consider how to address them. Listed companies are encouraged to ensure that their boards of directors are made up of a certain proportion of female directors, although these initiatives are voluntary.

Northern Ireland

All private sector employers with eleven or more employees (working more than sixteen hours per week) are required to register with the Equality

Commission. Specified public sector employers are automatically deemed to be registered, regardless of the number of staff.

All registered employers must submit monitoring returns on an annual basis giving details of the community background, sex and occupational classification of their workforce. Community background in this context means those who are treated as belonging to either the Protestant or the Roman Catholic community in Northern Ireland. All registered employers must provide details of their employees, applicants and appointees. In addition large private sector employers (those with more than 250 employees, full and part-time) and all public sector employees must provide details of promotees and leavers.

All employers registered with the Equality Commission for Northern Ireland must review the composition of their workforce, their recruitment, training and promotion practices at least once every three years in order to determine whether fair participation in employment is being secured by both Protestants and Roman Catholics (known as an Article 55 review). Where it appears to an employer in the course of a review that fair participation in employment is not being provided to members of one or other community or is not likely to continue to be provided, that employer is under a duty to determine and implement the 'Affirmative Action' (if any) which would be reasonable and appropriate for it to take and setting goals and timetables to assist in evaluating such affirmative action towards fair participation.

The Equality Commission can investigate the employment practices of any Northern Ireland employer at any time.

24.2. Checklist of Dos and Don'ts

- Consider whether to carry out equal opportunities monitoring to assess the diversity of the workforce and where improvements could be made.
- If monitoring indicates lack of equality then consider what measures may be taken to address this.
- Continue monitoring to assess whether the measures are improving diversity and whether further steps should be taken, and review progress regularly.

25. RESOLUTION OF LABOUR, DISCRIMINATION AND EMPLOYMENT DISPUTES: LITIGATION, ARBITRATION, MEDIATION AND CONCILIATION

25.1. Internal Dispute Resolution Processes

A grievance can be any concern, problem or complaint that an employee raises with the employer. Dealing with a grievance effectively can mitigate the risk of a tribunal claim.

The ACAS Code sets out key principles for handling grievances in the workplace. Most employers will also have an internal grievance procedure that incorporates the principles set out in the code. An employment tribunal may increase or decrease an employee's compensation by up to 25% for an unreasonable failure by the employer or employee (respectively) to comply with the ACAS code.

Generally, employers should try to resolve grievances informally. If a grievance cannot be resolved informally, the employee should raise it in writing with a manager (if the grievance concerns their line manager, the grievance should be raised with another manager or Human Resources). A failure to set out the grievance in writing does not absolve the employer from its obligation to consider the employee's grievance.

A chairperson should be appointed to consider the grievance and a meeting should be held to allow the employee to explain their grievance and how they think it should be resolved. The employee has the right to be accompanied to the meeting by a colleague or trade union representative. If the matter needs further investigation, the chairperson should consider adjourning the meeting and resuming it after the investigation has taken place. When the meeting is concluded, the chairperson should communicate its decision in writing without unreasonable delay, including (where appropriate) details of any action it intends to take to resolve the grievance. The employee should be offered the right of appeal.

In Northern Ireland, the employment relations service is the LRA, and it has its own code of practice should formal investigatory, disciplinary, or grievance action be required.

25.2. Mediation and Conciliation

Mediation is a process used for resolving disputes in which a third person helps the parties agree to a resolution. It concentrates on helping parties move from entrenched positions. The mediator, as a third party, manages or facilitates the process through which the parties get to a point where they can agree a way forward. However, the mediator does not impose any resolution.

As a precursor to any litigation in the employment tribunal, an employee must first contact ACAS (the independent arbitration, conciliation and advisory service) and engage in a period (typically one month) of mandatory pre-claim conciliation before any employment tribunal claim can be issued. ACAS will act as an independent conciliator to try to help the employee and the employer agree to a settlement and avoid litigation.

25.3. Arbitration

Arbitration involves an impartial outsider being asked to make a decision on a dispute. The arbitrator makes a firm decision on a case based on the evidence presented by the parties. Arbitration is voluntary, so both sides must agree to go to arbitration; they should also agree in advance that they will abide by the arbitrator's decision.

Arbitration can be seen as an alternative to a court of law with its rules for procedures such as disclosure of documents, evidence and so on. But arbitration is private rather than public. Unlike a court, in an arbitration hearing, the arbitrator will ask the questions. There is no formal cross-examination or swearing of oaths.

Arbitration is uncommon in an employment context in the UK, but is most often seen in collective employment-related disputes. For example, a trade union might be in dispute with an employer over the annual pay rise. The union could agree with the employer to ask ACAS to appoint an independent arbitrator from its panel of arbitrators to hear the two sides' cases and then make an independent and impartial decision.

Arbitration can also be used to settle individual disputes (although this is unusual). For example, an individual and an employer might decide to go to arbitration to avoid the stress and expense of an employment tribunal.

Statutory employment claims can only be settled by:

– using a valid settlement agreement which complies with certain requirements, including that the employee received independent legal advice on the settlement agreement; or
– using an agreement reached through ACAS, known as a COT3 agreement (available where a claim has already been raised with ACAS or brought in the Employment Tribunal).

Any mediation, conciliation or arbitration which results in a settlement, must be documented in a valid settlement agreement or COT3 agreement in order for statutory claims to be waived effectively.

25.4. Litigation

Most employment disputes must be brought in the employment tribunal, although certain contractual claims, often high-value ones, are often brought in the County and High Court (or Sheriff Court and Court of Session in Scotland). There are strict time limits that apply to employment tribunal claims, requiring most claims to be brought within three months of the act complained about. For certain claims, such as unfair dismissal, the employment tribunal is restricted as to the maximum compensation it can award.

25.5. Fines, Penalties and Damages

The tribunal has the power to award unlimited compensation in discrimination cases and compensation up to the lower of twelve months' salary or the statutory cap in unfair dismissal cases. Damages are calculated on a loss basis and, in most cases, the bulk of compensation is made up of loss of earnings. The employee is under a duty to mitigate any loss by seeking new employment.

As a general rule, each party usually bears its own costs in the Employment Tribunal, regardless of the outcome of the case. However, the Employment Tribunal does have power to award costs if it considers this appropriate, for example, where an employee has brought a claim which was misconceived.

25.6. Checklist of Dos and Don'ts

- Involve employees or their representatives in developing workplace procedures, and make sure those procedures are transparent and accessible to employees.
- Train managers on how to handle grievances effectively, when to involve HR, and how to spot when there may be a potential legal claim.
- Encourage managers to resolve issues pro-actively and informally before they get to a formal-grievance stage.
- Ensure that the grievance procedure is followed.
- Use a valid settlement agreement or COT3 agreement to settle employment claims.

26. EMPLOYER RECORDKEEPING, DATA PROTECTION AND EMPLOYEE ACCESS TO PERSONNEL FILES AND RECORDS

26.1. Overview

Employer processing of personal data relating to employees is governed by the EU GDPR and the DPA 2018. Processing personal data includes collecting, organizing, disclosing and storing data.

There are seven data protection principles which apply to the processing of personal data:

(1) Lawfulness, fairness and transparency: personal data must be processed lawfully, fairly and in a transparent manner.
(2) Purpose limitation: personal data must be collected for specified, explicit and legitimate purposes and processed compatibly with those purposes.
(3) Data minimization: personal data must be adequate, relevant and limited to what is necessary.
(4) Accuracy: personal data should be accurate and kept up to date.
(5) Storage limitation: personal data should be kept for no longer than is necessary.
(6) Integrity and confidentiality: personal data should be kept securely and protected from unauthorized access.
(7) Accountability: the employer is responsible for, and must be able to demonstrate, compliance with these principles.

Employers need to have a lawful ground on which to process personal data in relation to employees, and an additional ground for processing where the data is 'special category' data or data relating to criminal offences. Special category data is any information relating to an individual's racial or ethnic origin; political opinions; religious or philosophical beliefs; trade union membership; health; genetics; biometrics; sex life; or sexual orientation.

26.2. Personnel Files

As set out above, employers can only process personal data relating to employees on certain grounds.

The grounds on which employers may process personal data include: the employee's consent; to comply with the employment contract or a legal obligation; or for the employer's legitimate interests. It is usually not advisable to rely on consent, as it is unclear whether an employee can freely give consent, given the nature of the employment relationship, and also consent may be withdrawn. In most situations, the employer will be able to rely on one of the other grounds for processing.

If the information amounts to special category data or criminal offence data, an additional ground for processing is needed, and these include: the employee's specific consent or where processing is necessary in connection with an employment law obligation (and the employer has the necessary policy documents in place).

Employers must provide employees with information about the data they are holding in relation to them, the purposes for which they are processing the data, how long the data is kept for, whether the data is disclosed to any third parties, and the employees' rights in relation to the data. This information will usually be set out in a document called a privacy notice or a data collection notice, which is made available to employees, for example, on the intranet.

Employers are required to keep internal records of data processing, including records covering the purpose of processing, grounds for processing, details of any disclosures of data to third parties, and data retention periods.

26.3. Confidentiality Rules

Employee records should be kept securely, and only accessed by staff who need to see them, for example, the HR department or the employee's manager. Information should only be disclosed externally where there are grounds to do so, and employers should disclose the minimum information necessary.

26.4. Employee Access

Employees may make a data subject access request (DSAR) for information about the data their employer holds about them. An employer must respond to a DSAR within one month of receipt, although this period may be extended by two months for more complex requests.

The employer must provide details of all the information it holds in relation to the employee. The employee may request a copy of the information (and in practice almost always does). DSARs may be very wide ranging, for example, an employee may request copies of all emails in which their name appears.

There are some types of document which the employer does not have to disclose in response to a DSAR, including documents containing confidential information about third parties, and legally privileged documents.

If a DSAR is manifestly unfounded or excessive then the employer may be able to charge an administrative fee for responding, or may be able to refuse to respond. This might be the case if, for example, an individual made a DSAR and offered to withdraw it in return for a payment.

27. REQUIRED NOTICES AND POSTINGS

27.1. Overview

Modern Slavery

The Modern Slavery Act (MSA), which came into force in October 2015, sets out far-reaching reporting obligations on commercial organizations to address the role of businesses in preventing modern slavery and human trafficking in the UK.

The Act applies to commercial organizations, wherever incorporated or formed, that:

(i) are 'carrying on a business or part of a business' in the UK 'supplying goods or services'; and
(ii) have a total turnover, or gross receipts, of GBP 36 million or higher.

Organizations caught by the MSA are required to prepare and publish a report on their website on an annual basis outlining the steps they have taken during the previous financial year to ensure slavery and human trafficking are not taking place in their own business or in their supply chains.

The MSA provides the following as guidance on what should be included in an organization's anti-slavery statement:

(a) the organization's structure, its business and its supply chains;
(b) its policies in relation to slavery and human trafficking;
(c) its due diligence processes in relation to slavery and human trafficking in its business and supply chains;
(d) the parts of its business and supply chains where there is a risk of slavery and human trafficking taking place, and the steps it has taken to assess and manage that risk;
(e) its effectiveness in ensuring that slavery and human trafficking is not taking place in its business or supply chains, measured against such performance indicators as it considers appropriate;
(f) the training about slavery and human trafficking available to its staff.

Where the organization is a corporate body, the MSA statement must be approved by the board of directors (or equivalent management body) and signed by a director (or equivalent). Equivalent approval must be sought where the organization is a limited liability partnership or a partnership of any other kind.

An organization is then required to publish its slavery and human trafficking statement, written in easy to understand language, in a prominent place on its website. If an organization does not have its own website, it must provide a copy of its statement to anyone who requests it within thirty days of receiving the request.

Where an employer fails to produce a slavery and human trafficking statement for a particular financial year, under section 54(11) of the Act, the Secretary of State is able to bring civil proceedings in the High Court for an injunction or, in Scotland, for specific performance of a statutory duty. Continued breach would then be in contempt of a court order which can lead to unlimited fines being imposed on the organization.

Gender Pay Gap Reporting

Employers with at least 250 employees are required to report their gender pay gap annually, under the EqA (Gender Pay Gap Reporting) Regulations 2017. Employers are required to report each year:

- the gender pay gap, based on average hourly pay for male and female employees in the April pay period;
- the proportion of male and female employees in each of the four pay bands (quartiles) based on the employer's overall pay range; and
- the gender bonus gap, based on average annual bonus for male and female employees.

Employers are encouraged (although not required) to publish a narrative to explain the figures.

The employer's report must be published on the employer's website and also on the central Government gender pay gap website.

The Government has consulted on extending the reporting requirement to cover the ethnicity pay gap, and the response to this consultation is awaited.

27.2. Checklist of Dos and Don'ts

Not applicable.

28. BREXIT

The UK left the EU on 31 January 2020 (known as 'Brexit'), although the UK and the EU negotiated a 'Transition Period' to maintain the status quo until 31 December 2020.

Brexit is unlikely to have a significant impact on UK employment law. While many UK employment rights derive from EU law, most, if not all of these, have been enshrined in UK legislation and so they will remain unchanged. At the end of the Transition Period, there were some changes for UK nationals working for employers in the EU that become insolvent and also for businesses that have pan-European works councils. However, all other employment rights remain unchanged. The EU GDPR has been transposed into UK law as the UK GDPR.

In the longer term, there may be some scope for reform in some areas of employment law which are derived from EU law and which some commentators argue are unduly burdensome on employers. Possible candidates for reform which have been suggested include: the forty-eight-hour limit on working time; the rules on the accrual of holiday pay during sick leave; the rules on the calculation of holiday pay with respect to overtime and commission; the rules which offer equal pay and working conditions for agency workers; and the rules which do not permit harmonization of terms and conditions on a TUPE transfer. However, the UK Government has not given any indication at this stage that such reform is being considered.

In any event, the key impact of Brexit for UK employers is in relation to immigration, which is discussed in section 14 above.

www.ingramcontent.com/pod-product-compliance
Lightning Source LLC
LaVergne TN
LVHW021113300926
849160LV00009B/715
* 9 7 8 9 4 0 3 5 3 9 0 4 1 *